YOUR
BABY
CAN SWIM

ALSO BY BONNIE PRUDDEN

Bonnie Prudden's Fitness Book
How to Be Slender and Fit after Thirty
How to Keep Your Child Fit from Birth to Six
*Fitness for You (Library of Congress Talking Books
  for the Blind)*
Teenage Fitness
Fitness from Six to Twelve
Exer-Sex
Record . . . Keep Fit . . . Be Happy, Volume 1
Record . . . Keep Fit . . . Be Happy, Volume 2
*Filmstrip . . . Color . . . Sound . . . Manuals
  Keep Fit . . . Be Happy—Color/Cartoons*

*Available at the Institute for Physical Fitness,
Box 625, Stockbridge, MA 01262*

YOUR
BABY
CAN SWIM

BONNIE PRUDDEN

AQUARIAN PRESS®
A SUBSIDIARY OF THE INSTITUTE FOR PHYSICAL FITNESS
STOCKBRIDGE, MASSACHUSETTS

ISBN 0-9602146-0-7
Third Printing, 1979

To Lila and DeWitt Wallace
With gratitude and affection

CONTENTS

ACKNOWLEDGMENTS

Many people have a share in all our lives, yet who can recall the name of the lady who picked us up when we fell in front of her house that icy December day and taught us that a word of praise about our bravery was even better than candy for staunching tears? Who remembers which teacher it was who said, "You have a flair for this, you will do well with it some day."? And sure enough, we did. Who remembers the address of the person who wrote to us after we had tried so hard to push something through for the benefit of church, school, or town, and said "Well done."? Few of us do, yet ideas, words of encouragement, the contribution of some very vital information all come to us gratis at certain points in our lives.

That is how it has been with this book. Gratitude is due everyone who is mentioned in these pages, as well as to hundreds who are not: the mothers who week after week took babies to swim classes; the fathers who took time off from work to watch, to praise, and to join their children; the grandparents who conquered their own fears in order to help their children's children. And, of course, special recognition is due to the many dedicated teachers involved in baby-swim programs. While we will name only those teachers whose classes were photographed for this book, we would like to say "Thank you" to all those who contributed their insights and information.

The babies who swim so happily through these pages came from the classes of: Phyllis Brenner, Rockford, Illinois; Janet Chance, Newark, Delaware; Ann Coleman, Orlando, Florida, Hedy Cuculich, Chicago, Illinois; Barbara Denner, Painesville, Ohio; Mary Ann Durkin, El Paso, Texas; Jerry Hurkes, Chicago, Illinois; Joan Hungerford, Cheshire, Connecticut; Jane Swineford, Jamaica, New York; Judy Vachon, Leominster, Massachusetts.

YOUR
BABY
CAN SWIM

1
TALKING
WITHOUT WORDS

Your purpose in reading this book is probably to find out how you can help your baby learn to swim. The title assures you it is possible, and without question you will be able to do just that. A quick look at the photographs may give you the impression that such an adventure is a new frontier, and for millions it will be. A select few have enjoyed the experience for a long time. Now you and your baby can enjoy it, too.

There is more in this book, however, than the adventure of an infant's adjustment to a new environment, important as that is. We will also be talking about the basics of human relationships, about perception and sensitivity, both yours and your baby's, and about the many ways to communicate with babies.

In order to get the most from this book, and thereby give the most, you will need to rediscover a long-neglected quality within you. Eons ago, before man developed speech, he had this quality in abundance. When he lacked it, he perished. That quality is nonverbal communication. Once you have called upon it, exercised, and refurbished it, you will find you have a veritable "hot line" of communication. A little practice with babies, who are prime senders and receivers, and you will be able to "read" people as you never thought possible. By the time you have mastered all the lessons in this book, you will find a whole new dimension has opened up.

Building Bridges

Any strong emotion can be a bridge to another's mind. If you are in love you can *sense* what the loved one is feeling. If you are sharing danger with another, you can sense his fear or his courage, which in turn will affect your own reactions. Of course the antennae of some people are better than those of others, but anything in constant use will improve. The development of your ability to communicate nonverbally will be your fringe benefit in reading this book. For just as the baby who can swim has advantages over the nursery-bound child, so the person who can reach and be reached without a single spoken word has advantages over others.

If ever there was a time in history when communication was desperately needed, it is now. But words have a life of their own quite apart from the meanings we would give them. They wing from one mind to another like gulls through a changing sky. A gray gull left his mind, a white gull entered yours. That happens when only words are used. With nonverbal communication there is less margin for error, less chance of misunderstanding. The message goes directly from sender to receiver without the intermediate step of verbalization. You use several such methods of direct communication daily, probably without being aware of it.

The baby girl in the high chair looks across the table at you. You smile and wrinkle your nose. The baby smiles back, ducks her head, and peers out at you from under a tumbled bang. Your look said, "My, but you are a pretty baby." The returned look said, "I know it . . . and you're nice too." Had you spoken those words, they would have been lost on the baby—and you would have missed her reply.

Another form of nonverbal communication is touch. You are about to cross the street at a busy intersection. The small boy at your side is bursting with excitement. He sees the toy store on the opposite corner but he doesn't notice that the light has changed and the traffic has started up. You put a restraining hand on his chest and his attention turns to you and the approaching cars. Your hand said, "Wait, something has changed." Your warning was clear. Had you relied on words they might have been too slow.

Body movement also has a language of its own. It is almost always made unconsciously, but the sensitive receiver gets the message, even when it is not directed at anyone in particular. Your older boy stomps into the house the day the varsity list is posted at school. He throws his books into one chair and himself into another. No need to tell you his name wasn't on it. Or your teenage daughter walks slowly back from the mailbox, her shoulders slumped, her head down. No need to tell you there was no letter from Mike.

These forms of nonverbal communication—gestures and expressions—are already familiar to you. But there is more. *Feelings* are sent and feelings are received, even without conscious effort. How many times have you sat next to someone you didn't know and had a feeling of uneasiness? How many times have you felt that something was bothering a dear one? Nothing was said, yet you knew. And perhaps you even knew that it wasn't up for discussion. How many times have you been in a group and suddenly known that two members of that group were deeply and emotionally involved with each other? How many times have you said, "Oh, I don't like her, I can't say why, it's just a *feeling*"*?* Or perhaps you have been faced with the wonder of feeling close and warmly content with a complete stranger.

We all use *something* to help us reach out to others. With a little effort you can discover how people really feel about things—which is not necessarily the same as what they say they feel about things. You can hear calls for help that would never be spoken, and you can give comfort without ever knowing the details. You can give and receive strength, courage, and assurance. With the development of your innate sensitivity, you can do all those things—and you can talk to babies.

Babies Listen

Babies arrive in the world with all the parts of their magnificent mechanisms intact. They do not add an arm, a leg, an eye, a liver, a brain cell—or their incredible capacity for sensory perception—at some later date. Watch a new baby when different people hold him. Aunt Lulu, who has never had much of a life, lacks self-confidence. Her hands say, "Oh, it's so little, I hope I don't drop it." Holding the new baby sets up all kinds of jangling in her, and the baby jangles back with a howl. Lay the same baby in the arms of the waiting granny, who has raised four of her own, and the baby hears, "Oh how beautiful she is, so tiny, so perfect. . . . Just let me hold her close." And the baby responds with a nestling, head-turning movement.

When you talk to babies, either with thoughts alone or thoughts through words, babies listen. You may hear your own words and the baby may enjoy the sounds, but he *feels* the thought. Anyone planning to teach babies to swim must understand at the outset that what is thought is heard. Clutch at the black and the bleak and you will harm yourself and everyone around you. Harbor constructive thoughts and you build.

2
HOW DO
BABIES KNOW?

For young people today who are searching for a meaning, an answer—some proof that American Telephone and Telegraph is not all there is—thought communication does not seem so very far out. It is just such young people who are having the babies today, and they are willing to hear about the new doors that are opening in this area. One of these doors was opened by a man named Cleve Backster.

Learning from Plants

Cleve Backster works with lie detectors called polygraphs. One aspect of his work deals with untruth, which seems to be one of man's specialties, the other with plant and animal life, which knows only truth. Backster discovered that plants have other properties quite apart from photosynthesis. He decided to attach one of his machines to a plant in his office and found that the plant gave off electrical impulses just as people do. That was surprising enough, but it was only a small beginning.

A dog had the run of the lab and each evening Backster

used to put a raw egg in his food. The plants hitched to the polygraphs reacted violently each time an egg was cracked and opened. Was it possible that the plants knew that destruction had taken place? A record kept on egg breaking was compared with polygraph spikes and they matched perfectly. The plants did sense destruction. Every one of them reacted with great agitation.

Backster then began to wonder whether the plants might not be reacting to some action of his rather than to the slaughter, so he set up controlled experiments which would go on at night when no one was in the lab. At carefully timed intervals, live brine shrimp were dumped into boiling water. The plants registered their knowledge of death by setting up an electrical uproar each time.

Backster, whose training in detection made him wonder if plants could tell him anything about criminals, set up a mock crime and proved that, indeed, plants could tell him a great deal. Several of his students drew lots to determine who would enter the laboratory under the cover of darkness and destroy one of the plants. No one knew who had drawn the short straw. The following morning as the murdered plant lay in shreds on the floor the students paraded singly into the lab. There was no reaction whatsoever to those who were innocent, but when the guilty student entered, the surviving plants went wild. If plants can discriminate between people, is it surprising that babies can?

Learning from Babies

As Backster learned from plants, you can learn from babies. You, too, arrived in this world with your wonderful mechanism complete, even with the ability to share your mind with the minds of others. It will take some effort to revive this ability because most adults are a little rusty, but time and practice will render exciting dividends. There is no better sensitivity coach than a baby, whose sense receiver keeps him in touch with the world every hour of the day and night. There is no better classroom than water, which will give you every opportunity to strengthen your sending mechanism. Interdependency will be crucial and both of you will know it. Try to feel what the baby feels. Practice sending encouragement and admiration through your hands, your arms, your body, and your voice. Think for a moment what it would mean to you if the people you love sent you a steady stream of admiration and encouragement every day. Do you realize that you would have no recourse but to believe them?

Start your course in sensitivity by understanding your baby. To understand your baby, all you have to do is remember what it was like to be a baby.

3
WATER, WATER EVERYWHERE

It was warm where you were and there was water everywhere, in your ears and your nose and all around you. You had soft slippery walls to lean against and kick against. It wasn't pitch black, more like a blurry darkness, darker in winter and redder in summer if the sun shone on your container. It wasn't silent either. Long before you heard it, you felt the steady reverberations of a giant pump pulsing through your tiny sea. Something within you beat exactly twice as fast, and no orchestra ever held more truly to a rhythm. The feel and the sound was reassuring, a part of you. There were other sounds, too, gurgles and growls and sometimes, from far away, something you would one day call music. Your life was pretty ideal, and perhaps you felt it would always stay that way—but it didn't.

The Coming Storm

There was that first awful moment when the walls closed tight around you and the sound of the pump got louder as it hammered faster and faster. Your entire world was being shaken. You were learning the first lesson your body would teach you: outside happenings have the power to set up a tension storm within you. Then, as the clutch became all but unbearable, everything relaxed—the tremor passed. You had just composed yourself when *wallop*, there it was again. And with it came a second lesson: troubles come in bunches.

Tremor after tremor hit you in one wave after another. You bore the assaults, because there wasn't anything else to be done—and you waited for it to be over. It was an utterly terrifying experience, and one you would never get over entirely. Suddenly you wanted out, right away.

The World Outside

You began to bang your head against a seemingly solid wall . . . and slowly a door opened. One more furious clutch and you dove headfirst for the exit. Whatever was out there couldn't possibly be as bad as where you were —but it was.

Your tender little eyes, used to a dim watery glow, were attacked by piercing brilliance. You were seized in some sort of vise and literally pulled through. You were grasped by your ankles, head down and helpless, and for the first time you knew that there was such a thing as space that you could fall through. There was a sharp slapping sound, a feeling of pain you couldn't isolate, and a shriek. The whole event was insupportable, and your first sound was one of protest.

Fortunately, long before all the indignities of that memorable day could be carried out, you fell asleep. For the first time you learned there is a back door you would sometimes be able to take when troubles got out of hand.

Love Conquers All

Later, much later, you were moved again through that frightening space. But this time you were put down gently, and with a kind of magic, you knew somebody who loved you was there. How could you know that when you were so little? Because love is the most sendable message there is. Arms went around you and drew you close—and yes, there it was again, the strong, steady beat that had filled your hours, your days, your very being. All the rest of your life you would find satisfaction in rhythm, and unerringly, when you heard the beat of a drum, you would be able to make your fingers or feet beat just twice as fast. Your tiny mouth found something to work on and gradually the loneliness went away. Warm and close with the pump of life beating steadily near by, you closed your eyes and slept. Already you had learned something of struggle, loneliness, fear, pain, and love—and you were only one day old.

We could make life easier for new arrivals if we would only try to imagine that first day ourselves. Some grown-ups are not very good at imagining. This is unfortunate because the richness of a child's life will depend in large part on the richness of our imagination.

4
EXERCISE
AT ONCE

The last weeks in the uterus are very cramped. Arms are folded across the chest, contracting the pectorals and stretching the muscles of the upper back. The muscles of the abdomen are also contracted, as are those in the backs of the thighs and calves, which connect with the hamstrings. The lungs are collapsed and the chest is very small indeed.

Once in the world, babies should be encouraged to stretch cramped muscles and contract those that have done most of their growing in a constant state of overstretch. If you will compare the major posture problems of children—and grown-ups as well—with the state of the neonate's muscles upon arrival, you will find that those problems started in the womb: the soft abdominal area that shows up later as a potbelly; the contracted pectoral muscles and overstretched back muscles that go with being round shouldered; even the shortened hamstrings that can lead to backache. Such tie-ins make you wonder whether many a young person who at eleven or twelve develops a curvature of the spine may not have been leaning unnaturally to one side during those very important months in the uterus. You cannot begin too soon to counteract the effects of cramped quarters coupled with a sedentary existence.

The habit of taking exercise is not universal, but it can be developed. What is needed is a pattern that is adhered to without deviation—at the same time, in the same place, and with the same aids every single day.

The Place

The floor is the best place for baby exercises for several reasons. It provides good support and it puts the mother on the same level with her baby. It also provides a feeling of space. The baby's first days and nights are bound to be spent in confined quarters. Bassinets, cribs, prams, and arms offer security and warmth, but not a wide horizon. Then, too, there is always the hope that the mother who exercises her baby and is herself down on the floor where exercise is easily done will begin a program of her own.

Aids

A big towel makes almost any floor space acceptable. If the room is drafty an infrared bulb in a gooseneck lamp is ideal. It will keep the baby warm in almost any weather, and you can determine how much heat the baby is getting because it will shine on the back of your neck first. You will need a clock. Too much exercise on Monday leads to none on Tuesday. Limit your time to five minutes a session at first and if there is a record player handy, both you and the baby will enjoy timing movement to a good beat. Two bands of any pop record will do the job.

The Time

It really makes very little difference just when you exercise your baby, but you should try to conduct your "classes" on a regular schedule and at those times of day when you would ordinarily be changing his clothes or bathing him. This will eliminate unnecessary dressing and undressing. It should also be done when there is no chance of interruption, so take the phone off the hook.

Arm Stretches

When you are ready to start, undress your baby, and holding him very close, kneel down on the floor. Do not separate his body from yours as you place him on his exercise towel, but lean down with him. Only when his back is in contact with the floor do you take away that safe feeling of being part of you.

A baby has a natural self-supporting grip when he is born, and if you help him he need never lose it. Strong hands are a plus even for babies. Let him grasp your thumbs and close your fingers over his hands so that the grip is maintained. As you put pressure on his arms in exercises he will grasp more tightly. This reflex may be a holdover from some remote ancestor who needed it for survival. Like the swimming reflex (page 41), it comes with the baby, and like the swimming reflex, it *stays* with the baby as long as it is used.

Pull the little arms gently and slowly at first to a full stretch. In the beginning there will be some resistance. His computer hasn't been programmed for such action as yet. For a long time it will be harder for your baby to give up

tension in his muscles and relax them than it will be to contract them. This is also true of many adults. Unless they are taught to consciously relax their muscles, they suffer from many aches and pains, notably in neck, shoulders, head, and back.

When a baby's arm muscles resist stretch, he is working against resistance just as though your hands were barbells. He is building strength. When his arms stretch easily and long, he is developing flexibility. Either way you can only win.

Next, draw his arms across his chest. This movement stretches his back and exercises his shoulders as no random movement can. And *talk* to the baby. Your voice is new to him now but soon will be the pivot of his world. Give him the gift of your voice every chance you get, and remember it is the tone he hears. Sing to him too. Sing anything, in tune or out, the lyrics don't matter. Words like one, two, three, four may be just numbers to you, but to your baby they mean, "Here I am, here you are, here we are together . . . and I love you."

Do about eight arm stretches. Don't hurry. It's the complete all-the-way-out-and-all-the-way-in movement you are after. Set up a rhythm as soon as you can. He has it in him already. Remember your heartbeat all those months—and his heart beating just twice as fast.

When you have done the arm stretches to the sides eight times, then do the same number of overhead stretches. Draw the arms up over the baby's head and then down to his sides. Every time he reaches upward, his chest expands to make room for more oxygen. More oxygen means more fuel for body and mind. Also, using the lungs will make them steadily more efficient. (See Vital Capacity on page

123.) Also, the shoulder joints are introduced to a new position, one which the baby would not be able to attain himself for a long, long time.

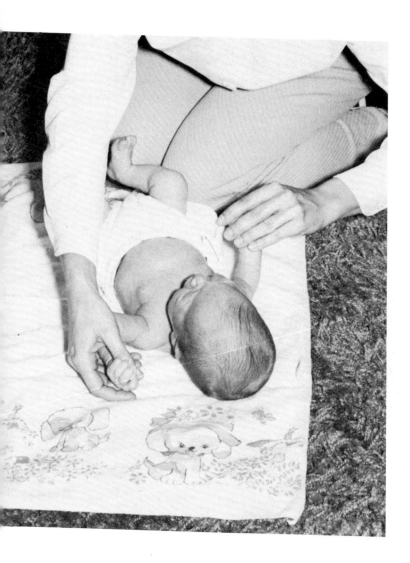

At first little babies do not make many movements involving one limb but not the other. Alternating one arm up and one down is a very advanced motion indeed. But you have a very advanced baby. Did you know that if you were to speak to your baby in one language, your husband were to use another, and his little sister a third, by the time he had learned to speak one, he would speak all three? Man uses only about one-tenth of his brain and the rest seems to lie fallow. Could that be because we don't develop more of it when we are just starting out?

Leg Stretches

Your baby's knees have been bent for months. Imagine how you would feel in a cramped back seat of a car if you were forced to ride from six to seven hours with your knees

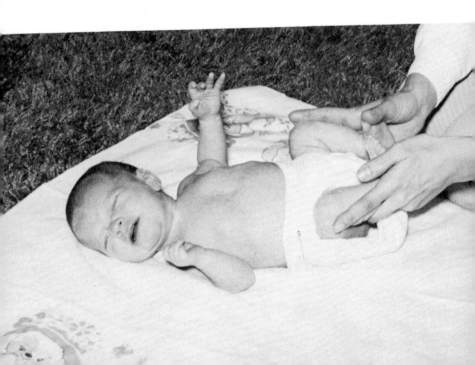

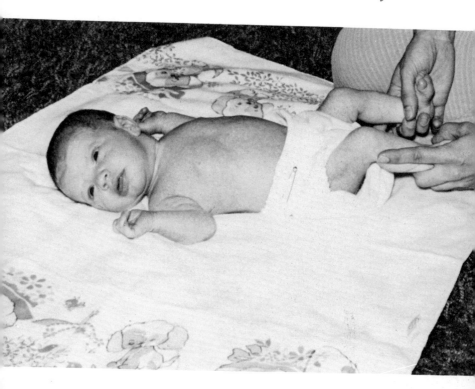

against your chest. Your first thought would be, "When can I get out of here and stretch my legs?" The baby likes leg stretches too. Do about eight of them, grasping the ankles and pulling gently out and back as pictured here.

The bicycle exercise is a real lifesaver, for it does the stretching that helps strengthen legs. The alternation of legs seems to counteract the natural contraction tendency, making extension of the leg easier and more complete. Furthermore, babies love it. Use this exercise to help you over rough spots in the doctor's office, in an airplane, when the baby is tired of lying in his crib, and just for fun.

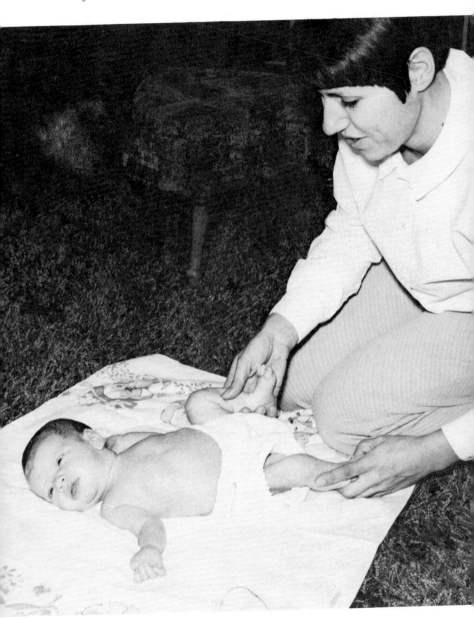

Pushing Ahead

No mother who has waited through those last two months of pregnancy is really surprised to see her baby push himself up into the corner of the crib or even halfway across

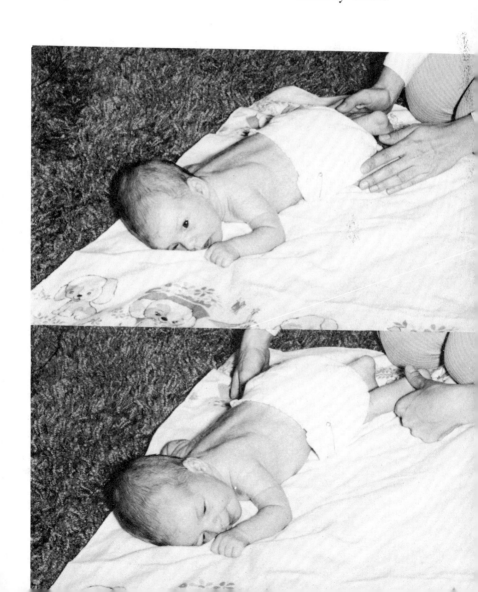

the room. There were several times during that waiting period when he got both little legs together and almost pushed her dinner back up. The only thing preventing most babies from practicing this activity is lack of leg room.

When you place the baby in the prone position, his legs will probably curl up under him. Place your thumbs against the soles of his feet and hold fast. There will be a mighty shove and the tiny body will move forward. Those legs are strong. Imagine trying to inch *your* body across a rough surface with just leg power. Pound for pound your baby would give you a good race. Try for two pushes at first and add whatever he wants to manage. The stretches are passive exercises, which means you do most of the work. Pushing across the floor is entirely the baby's decision and he does the work. As soon as he can locate objects, you will be able to encourage all kinds of floor progression by placing shiny articles a little ahead of him.

The Back Arch

Imagine how you would feel if some ill fate made it necessary for you to spend a night curled up in a child's crib. Long before morning you would be praying for a chance to straighten your back. The baby's back has been rounded for months. He likes new positions, so pick up the spindly legs and arch his back a little. Hold him that way for a slow count of three while making the appropriate noises that would go with such an adventure. For him it *is* an adventure. It probably would be for you, too, if two hands the size of wheelbarrows picked up *your* legs and arched *your* back!

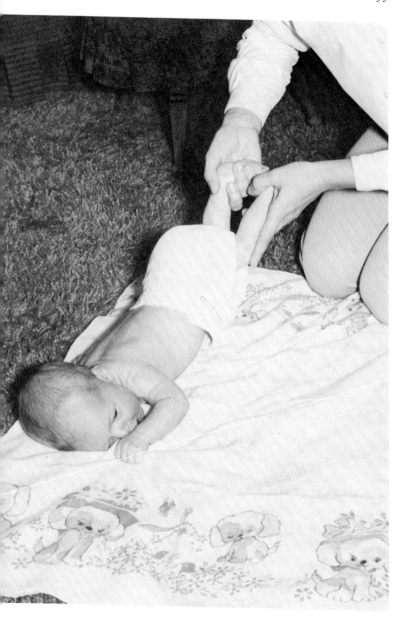

Now Is the Time

The whole series should take you roughly five minutes.
That's not very much time if you consider that a sixteen-
hour day contains 192 such five-minute segments. If you
change your baby's diapers eight times a day (a conserva-
tive estimate) you have him in readiness for this exercise
session eight times. Even if you take time for only six sessions, you will be giving your baby one half-hour a day of
delightful movement, and you'll never miss the time.

With that kind of regular activity the baby will eat better, rest better, and, most important, *feel* better. Babies
have stress just like the rest of us. It can come from being
too hot or too cold, from noise, or even from just lying still.
If you relieve that tension with physical activity you give
your baby a gift you could not possibly match with all the
presents you could buy. You give him the gift of a healthy,
attractive, strong, relaxed body. And if you start now, you
will get the greatest returns for the least time and effort.
For now is when the fastest growth is taking place. Now is
when all the foundations are being laid. Now is when
everything you do—or fail to do—has the most effect.

Nudists Are Nice

Incidentally, if you have a "summer baby," take him out-
doors occasionally to stretch and exercise. There's no feeling in the world quite like being naked in the sun. Not only
does the sun feel good, but it's good for you. It is a prime
source of vitamin D, which Adele Davis, who has written
a number of books on nutrition, calls the vitamin that sup-
plies beauty to children. Most foods lack vitamin D; the

sun provides it in abundance. But man's sun is very much like man's fire. Use it wisely and it will work for you, use it carelessly and you are likely to get burned.

When you take your little nudist out into the sun for the first time, think "redhead." For babies, like redheads, have extremely tender skin. There are many screening agents on the market that you can use to protect your baby, but a little common sense should also be used. Make your first sun bath a short one, and as the skin tans, you can stretch it longer and longer.

Vitamin D is absorbed through the oils in your skin. If you are at great pains to soap off all the natural oils you won't have much luck filling your body's needs. If you sun yourself without having washed off the oils but then pop right into a hot soapy shower when you go in the house, you will wash off the vitamin too, before your body has a chance to absorb it. Leave your skin in peace for a few hours. If you must take that shower because you are due at the Monday Muncher's Lunch Club at noon, do so, but know that all you got from your morning's sunning was a lovely time with your baby—which is nothing to sneeze at. Then try for your supply of vitamins the next day. If you live where the sun is a rare visitor, use a sun lamp, and use it every day.

5
LOVE
IN A TUB

Now that your baby is accustomed to exercise, he is ready to be introduced to water. You may start him as early as two weeks, but whatever the age, the success of your baby's water program will depend largely on you. One of the prerequisites is that you understand conditioning. In its extreme form conditioning could be explained like this: The child who is beaten by a drunken father will hide when he hears him and duck when he comes too close. The child who is accustomed to love, laughter, and caresses from a father, on the other hand, will run to meet him and joyfully reach for him when he approaches.

Your baby started his conditioning way back in the womb. He was conditioned to warm water which matched his own temperature. He was conditioned to the constant beat of your heart. He was conditioned to being closely held by something smooth and firm. It was a nice, untroubled time and he was perfectly comfortable. Now how do you make use of that?

Water Conditioning

The baby is already familiar with water; it isn't the water in the washcloth that makes him scrunch his face, it's the rough material and perhaps the manner of application. It isn't the water in the rubber Bathinette or enamel tub that sets him howling, it's the combination of chill air and the unprotected flight through space. When your baby is lowered into the tub, it isn't the water that's frightening. What is frightening is that the water doesn't cover *all* of him and that there is nobody else in there with him.

Position

There is another factor to consider, and that is position. In 1919 Dr. John Broadus Watson published a book called *Psychology from the Standpoint of the Behaviorist,* in which he included some observations on the behavior of infants. In tests on three newborn babies he found that when he immersed them up to their necks in the *supine* position, the reaction was as follows: "Violent expression of fear . . . a cry, checking of breathing, followed by deeper inspiration and rapid, entirely uncoordinated slashing of hands and feet." From that, Dr. Watson concluded that the newborn baby would certainly not qualify as a natural swimmer. The only support the baby could *feel* in that position, however, was Dr. Watson's hands under his back. The sensation under such circumstances would be akin to drowning.

Reflexes

In the late thirties, Dr. Myrtle McGraw did a more comprehensive investigation for the Normal Child Development Study of the Department of Pediatrics, Columbia University and Babies Hospital. It involved forty-two infants ranging from eleven days to two and a half years in a total of 445 observations. She found that when very little babies were placed *prone* in the water, with faces submerged, there was a marked swimming reflex—a definite rhythmic action not only in the arms and legs, but from side to side in the torso. The movements were forceful enough to propel the baby a short distance through the water. Newborns also exhibit reflex stepping and crawling motions, but she found that the swimming movements "are distinctly more synchronous and rhythmical."

Dr. McGraw discovered something else of great importance to our discussion: "Another outstanding feature of the infant's behavior during the newborn phase is breath control. Apparently a reflex inhibits his breathing while he is submerged, since he does not cough or show disturbances common among the older babies after they have been submerged." Dr. McGraw also tried submerging babies in the prone position but with their heads above the surface. While they did make swimming motions similar to the totally submerged babies, still "definite organization and rhythmicity of movements are . . . more pronounced when the infant is submerged." She felt also that the two reflexes, breath control and swimming movements, supported each other, since the swimming motions were more definite and pronounced when the breath was held. Dr.

McGraw found that after the age of about four months these helpful reflexes tended to weaken.

Nature had a reason for giving a neonate a grip in each little fist that can support his weight. He was expected to hold onto something, maybe his mother. The fact that he automatically holds his breath and automatically makes swimming motions when placed face down in water must mean something too. Perhaps at some time in our evolution we spent lots of time in water. In any case, the baby who is helped to use his fists through exercise keeps his grip and improves it. The baby who uses his inborn ability to hold his breath underwater and to swim continues to do both better and better.

Close Holding

Your heartbeat and your baby had everything in common for nine months. You can continue to use your heartbeat as a bond with your baby. Place his head close to your heart often, particularly before you take him swimming. It is one of the three things to which he is conditioned: warm water, close holding, and beat.

Babies love to be held, nobody argues the point. Babies who are never held are emotionally deprived. Babies who are held all the time, as they are in primitive societies, seem to thrive. In our society we fall somewhere in between. Not all our chores can be tended with a baby slung on our back, but many can. The baby packs and baby slings that have come into vogue in the last few years (there have always been some who used them) are giving babies more "holding" time, and it really doesn't seem to matter who holds them. So when it comes time to go into the water with your baby, your first thought should be *hold close*.

Taking the Plunge

With all of this basic and very positive information, you are now ready to take the plunge, but there is one further psychological factor to take into consideration.

Your baby has been conditioned to water, but you have been conditioned too—in a different way. Even if you have been able to swim the length of the pool underwater since you were ten, you will still have a qualm or two when it comes to taking your new baby under with you. You will need a backup for the first tub swim, both for moral and physical support. Choose your lifeguard carefully. Your baby will not only tune into your emotional state but your assistant's as well. If your mother thinks this is a great idea then ask her to help. If she is nervous or even slightly against it, invite a swimming friend. Teenage nieces are usually for it and they have an enthusiasm that babies enjoy.

With the choice of personnel settled, set the stage. First there is the question of warmth. If it is summer, there's no problem. If it is winter and you have a cool or drafty bathroom, buy an infrared bulb and use it to warm the room well ahead of the bath. Very hot water in the tub allowed to cool to elbow temperature will also help. You don't want the baby's computer to store a bit of information saying *water—cold*. It's too easy to take the next step—*no*.

Next there is the question of light. If your bathroom has an outside window and the "swim" is to take place in day-

time, you are all set. But if you have an inside bathroom
or you must do your swimming at night that is different.
Most bathroom lights are designed for shaving, plucking
eyebrows, and finding the first white hair. They do those
jobs well, but they also have a great deal in common with
that searing light of the delivery room. Assume that the experience has not been entirely forgotten and put a lamp
with a soft low watt bulb in one corner. There may be
some things that even you can learn about the connection
between light, bathing, and pleasant sensuality. You'll probably leave that soft light there forever.

Next, prepare the facilities. Wash out the tub and take a
shower yourself. Babies come with certain immunities, but
take ordinary precautions. Fill the tub as full as you can
with warm water (elbow test), and you are almost ready.
Now take the phone off the hook.

As you undress your baby talk to him. Wrap him in a
medium-sized bath towel and as you pick him up lean over
close so that your body touches the front of him before his
back leaves the table. The towel close around him plus the
proximity of you makes him feel safe. Soon he will feel
that you are the person who does nice things for him and
with him. The more you reinforce such feelings the easier
it will be to instill the trust that must develop if your baby
is to get the most from his relationship with you—and later
on, from life itself.

When all is ready give your baby to your lady-in-wait-
ing and sit down in the tub. As he is passed from one pair
of hands to the other, make sure he feels your face against
him before losing contact with hers. Leave the baby
wrapped in his towel till his body is underwater and he is
lying prone on yours.

If you are a large woman (the mother pictured on this page is five feet ten), you may have trouble getting all of both of you under the water. In that case just leave the towel across the baby's back. Now reassure your baby, as well as yourself, with the following thoughts:

1. You spent nine months in water and you liked it.
2. You remember how close and warm it was where you were.
3. We have been together a long time and we are going to enjoy this.

Next, slide down in the water so that the baby's body is submerged but his head, held against your breast so he can hear your heart, remains above the surface. Keep your head and his up by pressing the back of your head against the curving back of the tub and arching your back. There will be a little click in your baby's computer and out will come the information: slippery-close-water-pump-*wonderful*. The last thing you should think of is getting the baby clean. Leave the soap and washcloth outside the tub. Use your hands to rub his skin gently. And hum—flat or on key, the baby doesn't care, he likes the vibration and he likes you. You *feel* good.

About ten minutes will be right for the baby's first swim with you. Use every minute to fondle him and to reacquaint him with water, closeness, heartbeat, and skin contact. It is probably too much to ask that you repeat this every day, but at this stage give him (and yourself) that pleasure as often as you can manage it. After about five swims you will be ready to try submerging completely—head and all. He was ready in the first five minutes, it was your conditioning that had to be overcome.

Dunk Day

On your first "dunk day" it would be well to have that friend with you again, not for the baby's sake but for yours. Get into the tub with the baby and while you are puddling and paddling say the following things:

1. You were underwater for nine months. You liked it.
2. I like it underwater too.
3. We can go under together and it will be fun for us.

As you say these things over and over, remember that the baby hears and understands. Slide down in the tub as you did before, submerging just his body. Now, holding his head firmly against your breast so he can hear your heart, slide down further until his head is all the way under. While you are under, count to three slowly and then come up slowly. Once you break the surface there should be such a shower of praise and cuddling and laughter that there can be no mistake—the baby *did* something. He doesn't know what he did, but your reaction is unmistakable, and you can be sure he will want to do whatever it was again.

With combined action and praise you are establishing an important link of pleasure and expectancy between the two of you. A baby's life should be full of play, and this can only happen if he is lucky enough to have a playful mother. Studies show that playful mothers tend to provide a climate relatively free of conflict, which helps their children adapt more readily to life. If you never learned how to play, if life is all business and getting things done, stop a minute. Your baby will pay a price. If you never learned, then let him teach you. Your major investment will be time and attention. The returns cannot be calculated.

If by any chance your baby's breath-inhibiting reflex isn't as good as when he was first born, he may come up coughing and spluttering. Don't panic. It's the same thing that will happen a dozen times when his bottle delivers too fast. Do what you would do then. Pat him on the back, tell him how wonderful he is, give him a few minutes of water play, and repeat the dunking exactly as you did before.

You will be establishing a pattern, one he can count on always.

Here we go, one, two, three, *down*.
One, two, three, *up*.

6
MOTHER MAKES THE DIFFERENCE

In a book entitled *Major Influences on the Development of Young Children,* by Burton L. White and Jean Carew Watts, codirectors of The Harvard Pre-School Project, there is some valuable information which you can apply to your own situation. They found that what we might call "superior" children do not give evidence of their better adaptation to life before the age of ten months. Something, according to Burton and Watts, happens between ten and eighteen months that separates those who will have this advantage from those who will not. As you might suspect, it turns out to be the mother who makes the difference.

Their study showed that the mothers of these superior children were good organizers, designers, and rulers of their children's environment and that they were good "consultants," or advisers. They provided interesting materials for their children to play with, they did not stifle their curiosity by confining them in playpens for hours on end, and they took time to help them use the obstacles they encountered for growth.

Burton and Watts say that the babies of these mothers grow into children who can get the attention of adults for help and information. That's quite different from merely getting attention. The children anticipate consequences, plan and carry out projects, and understand quite complicated sentences. If this is accomplished between the ages of ten and eighteen months, what might happen to your baby if you start even earlier? Babies who are talked to learn sounds. Babies who are handled in many positions gain a kinesthetic sense. Babies who are moved and exercised to music develop rhythm. Babies whose skin is exposed to changes in temperature and environment are able to store more information in their computers than babies who suffer from unchanging confinement. And babies who can swim seem to be way ahead of others their age in a number of areas.

Crawling

When your baby can crawl he will want to try crawling with you in the tub. The mother who is a good consultant doesn't have to wait until the baby can understand her warnings: "Watch your foot, it's on the soap" or "No, you'll fall and hurt yourself." That lesson can only be learned by the baby through trial and error. What she can do is let him try his legs while keeping relaxed hands at the ready to prepare for any slip or spill. That's a good rule to follow with children in general. You cannot protect them from the bumps in life, but you can prepare them for many and even teach them how to avoid a few.

Prone

After several tub sessions you can begin to work for independence. When the baby is familiar with the ritual of slide-play-cuddle-dive-surface-smile-praise, put him prone in the water. With one hand support his chin and with the other, his tummy. You will be replacing the feeling of womblike closeness with the joy of kicking free. That's another good point to remember. When you want to change, progress, or prevent, don't snatch the child away from whatever it is that is holding his attention; present him with something different. Little minds retain everything, but they can really think about only one thing at a time. If your baby's mind is on catching a bumble bee and you hand him a shining buttercup that leaves gold dust on his fingers, he's bound to forget the bee.

If you can sometimes arrange your swims when daddy is home, he can help you to teach the little legs to kick, and you will be serving three purposes. The legs will get a needed lesson, you will start to forge a link of action and pleasure between the child and his father, and you will give that father a picture of shared loveliness he is not likely to forget.

All the Angles

Some babies like to sleep face down, some prefer their backs, and some curl up on their sides. Babies have preferences in the water too. You will soon learn which position pleases your baby the most because babies evince their pleasure with lots of action, namely kicking. Knowing the

preference is helpful because then you can make the right decisions. For example, suppose your baby has had a cold and has been out of the swim for two weeks. You start again by putting him in the position he likes. Or, he takes an unauthorized dunk and gets a mouthful. After the usual hugs-smiles-praise, begin again in the preferred position. But don't limit him to that position. See to it that he experiences every angle, then he can never be taken by surprise. Rely on the love and fun you share to get what you want —and what you want is a water baby.

Tub Float

Once the baby is used to various positions, he is ready to try floating on his back. Support his back at the shoulders. Most babies will curl at once into the fetal position. That is one reason for doing the back-arch exercise on page 34. The weight of the raised legs will send his bottom to the bottom. If you can get far enough behind him (see page 130) his head will have to tip back so he can find you with his eyes. This will help to straighten him out in the water. Try it yourself the next time you go swimming. First stretch out in the floating position, then bend your knees and raise your head to check on them. You will sink. Tip your head back and the rest of your body will stretch out unless you make a conscious effort to check it; you will be floating again.

It is important to try these things out on yourself for two reasons. First, you will be better able to understand your baby's actions and reactions. Then, too, your body is a wonderful laboratory in which to rediscover the many sensations that affect you daily. What do things feel like?

What is the difference between a shag rug and a Persian? What is the difference in temperature between grass, marble, and wood? How rough is the cement walk, the macadam in the driveway, and the bricks on the patio? Mostly we are too busy or too preoccupied to feel the world around us and we miss a lot. Babies are busy too, but they are busy *feeling*. Imagine what newly cut grass must feel like as it sticks to his wet little feet. Imagine what the sun-warmed tile feels like, or, better still, take off your shoes and find out.

A New Kind of Dunk

When you are ready to try something a little different, sprinkle the bottom of the tub liberally with red and blue poker chips. Start with the familiar—the sliding play, the praise, the close-hold dunk. Then rest the baby in the prone position on your closed legs. Use the old formula: "Here we go, one, two, three, *down*." Get your legs out of the way and press the baby down so that the water covers as much of him as possible. It will feel different to him, but before he can react to his new situation, something else will attract his attention: "What's that down there?" You may close your eyes when you go underwater, but the baby doesn't. With the poker chips you will have created a new and exciting experience. It is at this stage of life that you foster curiosity and the spirit of adventure.

Each new adventure must have something going for it. In this case it is color and mystery. Let the baby stay down as long as he usually does in the close-hold position, then bring him up and reach down and get a poker chip for him. Each time you do that you will be rewarding his dive, and

one day he will reach out when he is down there and pick one up for himself. Don't worry if he wants to stay down longer than you think he can or should. His instincts will tell him when he should surface.

Once the baby has become intrigued with what he can find on the bottom of his pool, you can remove yourself a little. It will no longer be necessary to get wet *every* time. But do get back in from time to time just for the simple pleasure of being close.

Tub or Pool?

There are advantages to giving the baby his first swimming lessons in a bathtub rather than a pool. To begin with, it often takes time and effort to get to a pool, so the lesson usually is restricted to once a week or so. A baby can forget a lot in a week. The more often and consistently he can be exposed to water, the more ingrained those beginning reflexes will become, and soon they will be a part of him that cannot be lost.

There does come a time when the tub, like the amniotic sac, becomes just too small or the baby becomes so proficient and adventurous that it's time to move on. Then a pool must be found. This does not mean you should give up tub swimming. Water is a child's most delightful toy and is far more exciting than a playpen, fenced off area, or a walk in the park. It can even take the place of swim class at the pool when inclement weather or holidays cut into swim programs. Even if you were to keep up your tub-swimming dates together just once a week, you would be gaining credit that can never be equalled again. If a year and a half is the cutoff age for laying the foundations, attitudes, and patterns which are to last a lifetime, then you have a chance at seventy-eight investments in a lifetime.

7

NOTHING NEW UNDER THE SUN

The idea that babies can swim is not new. Reports brought back from the South Seas by early American whalers tell of babies being washed in warm pools immediately after birth. It should come as no surprise that such babies kicked their feet and made swimming motions when their heads were immersed. What could be more natural to a people who used the warm Pacific waters for their livelihood as well as pleasure than to take new babies into their baths with them? As we have seen from Dr. Myrtle McGraw's studies, neonates swim very well when immersed and prone. The English biologist Allistair Hardy, who has also done studies on neonates, found that when newborn babies are placed on gently tilted ramps so that they can work their way down into water without help from human hands, they will swim without assistance or panic. The South Sea Islanders of two and a half centuries ago would not have found this at all surprising.

More recently, in October of 1967, it was reported that

in Hawaii a tiny baby named Anneke Pickering, who was born two months premature, was given her first swim in the warm sea at the age of five days. There was really very little difference between the sea and the shelter she had left too soon. It was brine and it was warm, which is far more natural than a hospital incubator. Anneke only weighed five pounds, but she loved the water and thrived in it. Perhaps premature babies might do a better, quicker job of catching up if they were bathed in a little warm salt water occasionally.

In Australia, a man named Forbes Carlile, an Olympic swimming coach, began some time ago to train a squad of babies for the 1984 Olympics. He opened the pool to two-month-olds believing that you cannot start a child too young if you want to produce gold-medal winners. There is no way of knowing right now if those little Australian hopefuls will ever win any medals, but not one baby will have wasted his time. Any skill learned early becomes more than a tool; it becomes a part of you. All Carlile's babies will be fine swimmers, which is a great asset in a country where ninety percent of the population lives within one hour of the beach.

Water Babies

Not all baby swimmers are from faraway lands. We have our own "water babies" at Cypress Gardens in Florida. It all started when a woman named Jen Loven gave her grandson his first swimming lesson before he was nine days old. When granddaughter, Julie, came along she had to wait until the tenth day of life before she could begin. But Julie was no slouch; when she was nine weeks old she could hold her breath and kick herself for a distance of ten feet all by herself.

My own experience with water babies began in the pool at the Westchester Country Club in Rye, New York. One minute my thirteen-month-old daughter, Petie, was crawling at my feet as I watched a diver practicing from the tower, the next she was off like a wobbly kitten after a butterfly, over the edge and going down. For one frozen second I watched her sink. It seemed like forever before I could make myself move, but in that "forever-moment" my mind took in a picture I only really saw later: that baby was smiling. There she was, with her eyes wide open and a huge grin on her face. I took off into the pool, fully dressed, slipped in under her, and brought her to the surface. I expected to hear shrieks of terror if not a strangling cough. Instead, she blew out a mouthful of water like a tiny whale. Then she stuck her tongue out to taste her upper lip, and before I could push her to the side of the pool, she was patting the surface and laughing at the splashes.

As with most mothers when their offspring survive something they consider dangerous, my first reaction was fright, then relief, and finally annoyance. I wasn't annoyed with the baby, however, but with myself. Why had I been so dumb? That baby could have been swimming for months instead of splashing about in a rubber wading pool. The very next day Petie's lessons began with a trip across the pool holding onto my straps. She was delighted. Long before she could walk with assurance, she could swim in ten feet of water. She liked to jump into the pool, holding hands with me, and soon she could be left on the bottom to surface by herself and then paddle to the ladder.

Learning to Trust

Until then I had forgotten that my father had taught me to jump off the high diving platform long before I could really swim. He would be down there treading water and say, "All right now, jump; I'll catch you." He'd reach out and grab me after the splash and haul me up. If I jumped past him and went deep I never worried; he'd be right down after me. He had said he would catch me and I believed him. That was the key: I trusted him.

Erik Erikson, in his book *Identity, Youth, and Crisis*, says that the amount of trust a baby absorbs from his early experience doesn't seem to depend on such essentials as the amount of food or even attention a baby is given, but rather on the quality of his relationship with the parental figure. Somehow a sense of trustworthiness must be established. There are many ways of doing this, but I wonder if the sharing of potential danger (in a controlled situation, of course) might not hurry the miracle along a little. "I am here," says the mother. "She is near," says the baby. Such a blending of reassurance and confidence invariably contributes to trust—and that trust forms a sort of magic, untouchable core that one day will be translated into the feeling, *"I am here and I know who I am."*

The tiny South Sea Islanders swam because all South Sea Islanders swam. I swam because my father swam (and also because my mother, who couldn't swim, was determined I should never suffer the fear that went with her into the sea). What happens to children who have two parents who can't swim? Two-thirds of the people who drown never learned to stay afloat even under ideal circumstances. Certainly mothers who cannot swim must endure a certain amount of tension when they see their children in water. Many professional swimming teachers who have worked with babies have strict rules pertaining to mothers, tactfully but definitely saying, "Get lost." If the mother is a very tense and anxious person that rule might apply, but as a general prohibition it would certainly limit the number of babies who could be taught to swim. Furthermore, it would prevent the construction of a very valuable bond between mother and child, a strong bridge which is the more resilient for having been built while sharing a hostile environment.

8
HOW DO
YOU START?

If you wanted to teach thousands, even millions, of babies to swim, what would you need? You would need teachers, not by ones and twos, but by thousands and millions. Where could such a number be found? The answer is obvious. For almost every baby needing to be taught to swim there is a handy, ready, and willing coach, his mother. True, many mothers couldn't keep chin above water themselves and might be terrified if they had to "dive" with a real live baby. Some might even prevent their babies from learning by unwittingly throwing up a wall of tension which the baby couldn't scale. But on the plus side, many babies would have a great experience and so would their mothers.

Just an Idea

After my own success with my daughter Petie, I began to ponder the idea of sharing this wonderful experience with others, bringing mothers and babies together in a situation where they could learn to swim together. But where? How? There was only one way to proceed and that was to take the first step: find a pool, a teacher, a mother, and a baby. I knew, of course, there would be many obstacles to overcome—not the least of which would be public opinion.

I first discussed the idea with Charles Swineford, general secretary of Detroit's Northeastern YMCA, in the late fifties. He was receptive and enthusiastic, and we immediately began outlining a plan of action. But convincing the other members of the Y of the soundness of our concept was another matter. Who ever heard of babies in a YMCA pool? It was difficult to sell such an idea then, just as it had been almost impossible for me back in 1947 to sell the idea that American children were becoming soft and needed exercise. I realized then that if you have an idea you believe in, it does no good to wait for a foundation to fund you—many good ideas would wait forever. You have to find a way to get started by yourself.

Charles Swineford found a way. He simply staged a little impromptu "class," with his wife, Jane Swineford, a young mother named Maryann Cook, and her infant daughter, Cheryl. Into the YMCA pool went the three, and into the *Detroit News* Sunday Supplement went the story—complete with pictures. The YMCA telephone began ringing immediately and has hardly let up since. Mothers from all over the area wanted to know how they could enroll their babies in the class.

From Little Acorns

Since that day, they have not been able to supply enough space or instructors to keep up with the demand. From the Y's standpoint there was another benefit, since the diaper-swim-and-gym program, as it came to be called, could make use of space, which had been lying idle most of the time, from nine in the morning to three in the afternoon.

At the end of two years, Detroit's Northeastern YMCA was serving five hundred youngsters a year, grossing fifteen thousand dollars and netting seven thousand dollars. This was a bonus we hadn't thought too much about in the beginning. At the end of five years they were grossing forty thousand dollars a year and netting twenty thousand dollars.

From those humble beginnings Ys all over the country are now serving the preschooler. Most of the instructors are trained by the Bonnie Prudden Institute for Physical Fitness, in Stockbridge, Massachusetts, a training program I began in 1947. Over the past fourteen years I personally have visited some 420 cities, giving baby-swim demonstrations in Ys, health clubs, and other institutions, which have in turn begun programs of their own. According to Mr. Swineford, there has never been a dissatisfied parent who has been in a Y class with one of our instructors. The secret, of course, lies in the fact that only people who really want to teach babies come to the Institute to learn, and what you really want to do, you do well.

In 1971 the Swinefords transferred from Detroit to the Eastern Queens YMCA of Greater New York, which had not had any preschool classes since starting almost twelve years ago. It was no trick at all to get a class going, and today they serve one thousand children a year, with a waiting period of one year. (You sign up the day the pregnancy test comes in positive!)

Why Join a Class?

Not only will you and your baby become proficient more quickly in a class, but you will share excitement and sociability with others. Such sharing is not only good for babies, it's very important for mothers. Once the baby arrives, many young women find themselves alone with that baby for most of their days. That is one of the more devastating things that happens to women with small children: isolation. If they could just get out and share time and experiences with other women, everybody, including the baby, would feel better.

Where Do You Look?

At the present time the YMCA and YWCA provide most of the baby-swim programs, but at this writing more clubs, recreation areas, schools, and so-called spas are opening their doors to babies. Even hotels and motels are being invaded by lilliputians. The advantage, for the moment, goes to the Ys; because most of their teachers have been well trained, their pools can be heated to eighty-five degrees, and their filter systems must pass regular inspections.

But suppose there is not a Y in your town, no teachers, and only you seem to be interested. First look around for a pool. You'd be surprised at the number that are nearby and largely unoccupied. If you find one and can talk the owners into letting you use it for a few brief periods a week, then look around for three friends with babies and suggest they join you. If you have been tub swimming for a while you'll have little difficulty persuading your friends. Just invite them for a look at what *your* baby can do. Or lend them this book. The reason for the three friends is the same as for the assistant at your first tub swim and dunk. Everybody needs bolstering. This applies even in your own backyard pool.

Whether you are a complete amateur, a mother with no thought for any baby but her own, or a full-blown professional, the next pages will give answers both to your questions and to those who question what you are doing.

9
FACING
THE CRITICS

When you start something new you have to expect people to take pot shots at you. Your only protection lies in a firm conviction that you are right. Even if you plan to teach your own baby to swim in your own pool in your own backyard, you will get lots of criticism. There are neighbors, mothers, mothers-in-law, husbands, and even occasionally a doctor who may object. None of them will be able to stop you if you really want to do the job. But it helps to be prepared with some hard facts.

Ammunition

America is leisure country. Almost any northern hill worth the designation sports a ski tow, cross country trail, or snowmobile track. In summer the national parks turn into one huge camp ground. Motorboats clutter the lakes and bays in menacing profusion. There's at least one backyard pool in almost every neighborhood, apartment complex, or condominium. Wheels have brought water within reach of just about everyone—whether or not they are capable of handling themselves in water.

According to the National Safety Council, drownings were the third leading cause of accidental death in the United States in recent years. That figure is rising steadily as more and more people have more and more time to spend in leisure activities.

Over sixty percent of those who drowned were young people under the age of twenty-five, and the greatest number of drownings was suffered by the fifteen- to nineteen-year-olds. Most of the casualties were boys, and two-thirds of them did not know how to swim. The Joint Committee of Physical Fitness, Recreation and Sports Medicine, in a recent statement, said that "children under the age of three are the most vulnerable." So vulnerable are these little people that the committee felt "organized attempts to reduce the toll are indicated." It has been suggested that one positive step be taken by fencing in water hazards. While about forty percent of the drownings occurred when people were swimming or playing in water, it seems only five percent happened in pools which might conceivably be fenced. Seventeen percent occurred while people were boating and thirty-nine percent were due to falls from shores, docks, bridges, etc. It is virtually impossible to fence a shoreline. Here again, we cannot *protect* a child, or an adult either, from the perils of the world. We can, however, *prepare* people of almost any age to meet them with a good chance of handling them successfully.

From the above study, it would appear that children between birth and three years of age should get first consideration, since they are the most vulnerable. An organized and concentrated effort to teach this group to swim now would mean that by 1987, as the boys in that group begin to reach the age when they have greatest access to water (and therefore greatest susceptibility to drowning), the loss of life would be drastically reduced. Presumably as girls attain more freedom, they too will be increasingly exposed to the perils of drowning. Teaching them to swim as babies may serve to keep their heads above water while they strive for the freedom to share the perils, as well as the pleasures, of their male peers. And we can be sure that no baby girl who has been taught to swim will later overlook *her* baby's water education. There is no reason for a child to drown if there is a bathtub in the house or a single swimming pool in town.

Is Water a Hazard?

Pools, rivers, lakes, and bays are often considered to be water hazards, but many people give little thought to ditches, cisterns, cesspools, and construction holes. A child unfamiliar with water can drown in a gutter after a rain storm. It would seem sensible, then, to familiarize very young children with water rather than hazards. If you can swim you do not need to ask yourself what sort of water hole you have fallen into. The same stroke will be used in sea, quarry, or canal, with the same object—to get out.

It has been suggested that mothers who attend swim classes with their babies might overestimate the abilities of their children, thinking them to be "drown-proofed." There is no better way of learning the exact limits to any child's abilities than to spend one or two half-hours a week in a pool alternately dunking and rescuing him. The object of a baby-swim class is to condition the children to stay afloat in water, and not make a decision as to the potential dangers connected with a given situation. Obviously not even fifteen- to nineteen-year-old boys can manage that.

Panic and Self-Control

Almost anyone can be taught survival techniques that will protect him from drowning. What is required is some simple know-how and self-control. Panic is the great drowner of children, who are sometimes found face down in wading pools hardly deep enough to cover their knees had they been standing. Self-control is a by-product of positive habits and self-confidence. Self-confidence is developed by amassing a host of successes, and whether those successes are large or small makes little difference. It is the climate that counts. To present this a little differently, if you want to destroy self-confidence in a child, see to it that he fails. Criticize him, complain to and about him. Call attention to his mistakes, carp, and scold. Sneer at him and jeer at his every effort. You will not only destroy his self-confidence, you will ruin his life. Praise him, and you will be fostering self-control.

Viruses

It has been charged that swimming babies would be "subject to significant exposures to enterviruses, adenoviruses, and other potentially dangerous microorganisms." In the fifteen years since the Detroit Y started its baby program there has not been a single such case, and they have taught many thousands of babies. Nor have we had reports of such problems from any other Y. (See questionnaire on page

237.) This fine record is probably due to the watchful eye that the public health department keeps on the disinfecting of public pools. In 1957 The U.S. Public Health Association recommended that all long-haired bathers wear caps because hair is known to carry staphylococci and other microorganisms. Now, however, the ordinances and regulations covering public swimming pools are such that the water must be of "drinking water quality," and last year the bathing cap was dropped as unnecessary.

A Question of Aesthetics

Another objection to babies swimming is that "incontinent infants in pools certainly pose an aesthetic problem." That presumably means they might have bowel movements during a class. In thirty-two years of baby swims I have never known this to happen.

There is, however, a strong probability that the babies will urinate during the session. There may be some who view this as a legitimate reason for not teaching them to swim, but it doesn't hold water, so to speak. Tests done in many Ys before and after baby swims, juvenile swims, and adult swims have shown that modern filter systems can handle anything produced by tiny bladders. They are, after all, geared to take care of much older children—and even adults. Backyard pools are more vulnerable, but the proper use of your test kit will assure you of clean water.

The Sick Baby

There is one precaution you should take. A sick baby may not pass on germs to other babies in a pool, but a sick baby put into a pool can get sicker. He certainly wouldn't be up to the experience, and that could easily tie the feeling of being miserable to water. If the baby is fussy, even when the cause is only teething, it is better to miss a day, or several days, if necessary. But keep in mind that you will have to start from the beginning again. Whenever classes are interrupted, even for holidays, you should begin again. The wise teacher goes back to grade one after vacation and brings her pupils rapidly through the familiar to the new. By so doing she reinforces the foundation, builds confidence, fills in weak or missing links, and gets everybody ready for what's next.

Did You Ever Teach Hopscotch?

Good teachers are born, not made. If you find it easy to communicate your ideas to others, if you can communicate enthusiasm, if you can break down complicated things into simple steps, you have the makings of a teacher. Any kid who could teach another kid to play hopscotch has those makings.

If you have the inclination to teach, you could do no better than to start with babies. Babies are grateful and cooperative and they don't criticize. If you know what to teach and use reliable materials and methods, you can start a baby-swim class. At first you may be unsure of yourself and your results may not seem very impressive. But as the routine becomes familiar and the teaching patterns are established, both you and your tiny pupil will develop self-confidence.

Whether you are to be a teacher of one, working alone in your backyard pool, a leader of three mothers teaching their babies at the Ramada Inn pool, or an instructor of a baby-swim class at the local women's club, athletic club, recreation department, or Y, the following pages will show you how it can be done. It won't take you long to add innovations of your own. You may even find better ways of doing things. The directions given here work. They have been tested over a period of three decades, and you can feel on solid ground with them—even in water.

10
TEACHING
MOTHER

If you are dealing with only you and your baby, just reading this material should be enough to get you started. If you are teaching a group, however, you should meet with the mothers alone the first time. The lesson should be for *them*. Let's take the biggest and most unwieldy group for our example, let's say you are teaching a large class at the Y or a club.

The First Session

Give your mothers all the information you have just read, with a list of the major points to take away with them as a reminder:

BABY-SWIM SHEET

1. Your baby has been in warm water for nine months; swimming is a familiar condition to him.
2. The younger the baby, the better he "remembers."

3. Newborns have two important reflexes: they make swimming motions with their legs, arms, and torso, and they hold their breath when face down in water.

4. If you use those reflexes to teach them to swim, they will not lose them.

5. You can impart your tension to your baby, so try to relax and enjoy your classes together.

6. The baby may do some screaming the first few classes. Don't be alarmed. What did he do the first time you gave him a bath?

7. He may ship some water at some time and cough and splutter. Do the same as you do when he gets water too fast from a bottle.

8. If you must miss a class for any reason try to go tub swimming with your baby at home.

9. Some babies are slower to learn than others, but all babies can learn to swim. Patience and consistency are the key.

10. Do not limit your activities to water. Your baby's exercise program should start when you bring him home from the hospital.

Nothing to Fear

When you meet with the mothers the first time, find out which ones are swimmers, which cannot swim, and which, if any, are afraid of water. If you discover that one is really terrified and that she is coming to class to try and save her baby from such unreasoning fear, you have a problem, but it is not insurmountable. Unfortunately, it is not enough to want freedom from fear for a child. If the mother harbors fear the child will sense it and adopt it for his own. You will have to do a double job. Try to arrange a stand-in for the mother for the first month. There are many women who like water and babies and would just love to help. But don't let the real mother off the hook. Ask her to bring a large rubber doll to class the first time she brings her baby. The stand-in will work with the baby, while the mother will go through exactly the same motions with the doll. If the child is old enough to know that the mother is near, it will be wise to send her to work with some other mother-baby team where her baby can't see her. It will take a little time, but the mother will become accustomed to the water and to her baby's reactions.

Worth the Effort

You will find, after that first class, that those who came only out of curiosity or because a friend talked them into it may drop out. Those are the ones who will drop out of anything once the novelty has worn off. They will realize that it is going to take a lot of energy to join a baby-swim class. The mother must gather her baby's equipment, get to the car or bus and cross town with him, undress him and herself, and then repeat the whole thing in reverse. And it means participating. Some mothers just don't have that kind of energy. The mothers who return after the first session, however, will probably come back for a third and fourth, and many will stay on until their babies grow into classes for older children.

You might mention an added benefit to your mothers. Every minute they spend in the water working with their babies, they are burning calories. Also, as they move about they are doing resistance exercises with their legs. If you can provide music for your classes they will enjoy moving to the beat.

What to Wear

At this point the discussion of swim wear should be undertaken. Most of the programs have given up on diapers; they get soggy and give the baby a feeling of being dragged down. Most babies wear swim suits or training pants. Mothers should wear brightly colored suits, as babies love color. Also, it is best to wear the same suit for all classes. Bikinis are better than full suits because babies like the feel of skin. The water should be at least eighty-five degrees for babies, but if you can't attain that temperature then they should wear little shirts for extra warmth.

How to Hold

Have the mothers sit on the edge of the pool, as they would if they had their babies in their laps. Show them with a rubber doll exactly how they will hold their babies as they walk about in the shallow water bobbing up and down and talking to their babies and each other. Stress the importance of making it a pleasant social occasion.

Demonstrate the *heartbeat hold*, the baby's body pressed gently against the mother's in an upright position, the little head held close to the breast so he can hear the reassuring sound of the familiar pump. Remind the class that the bobbing should be done gently at first so that the baby will feel the motion but not get water splashed in his face. Explain the importance of friendly noises and of group reinforce-

ment. You should bring up the problem of babies who cry. Tiny babies rarely cry when introduced to water. The greatest criers are little boys aged two. Usually there will be anywhere from one to several children who will cry the first two or three lessons and then it stops. Once in a while every baby in the pool will set up a howl, but fortunately such times are rare. It is wise, however, to warn the mothers so they can expect it and not take fright if theirs is one of the howlers.

What to Bring

Each baby will need a large towel which can be wrapped around him during the class if he gets cold and has to be taken out. If the child is several months old and has a water toy, it should travel with him. Most mothers have baby tenders (page 98). Have them bring them so that each child can be assured of his own little "lounge" while his mother is dressing, taking a swim, or working in an aqua-exercise class. You might also mention that the babies will be ravenous after their swims, so the mothers should provide accordingly. With that last bit of information it's *here we go, one, two, three!*

11
NOW
BRING BABY

You will need one or two assistants for the first lesson so that the mothers will be able to get into and out of the water without carrying the babies.

Pick a Baby

Start with the pool-edge sitting position, each mother holding her own baby. You can borrow one for demonstration purposes. Try to pick one belonging to a placid mother. If the baby is facing away from you (even if he has reached the critical age of six months when he really knows to whom he belongs), he will probably accept you. But to be safe, try to select a very young one. The bright lights, the shimmer on the water surface, the presence of many people, even the room itself with its atmosphere of excitement and pleasure will keep him intrigued. A little water allowed to dribble down his legs and tummy keep him occupied. The feel of the warm body against his back, the skin under his legs, and that reassuring arm around him all add up to

good. Get all your verbal instructions across to the mothers *before* you start with the baby. Nobody likes shouting in his ear.

Get Your Feet Wet

Take the baby into the pool and hold him close as you proceed with the demonstration step by step. Talk softly to him and bob gently up and down, moving from shallow to deeper water until it covers your body almost to shoulder level. Show the mothers how they will be able to bend their knees a little and bring the water right up to the baby's neck, when they are in the deeper water. They will see that you have complete control. There are no sharp drops in swimming pools and the anxious mother need have no fears about getting in over her head.

And If It Rains

If one little mite runs into trouble, be prepared. Sometimes
the water feels cold to the baby or he takes too big a swallow or in the excitement clouts himself in the eye. Or
maybe he just feels like complaining. The only way he can
voice his complaint is to yell. This is natural. Your attitude
toward the baby should not be "Oh, you poor dear, darling
baby, what a terrible thing to have happen." He's already
got that idea. No, you should do just what you would do
if his mother lost the top of her bikini, laugh to show it is
not such a serious matter. Then try to distract his attention.

It helps to keep a couple of poker chips somewhere in your suit which can be conveniently tossed into shallow water and "found" with the baby's help. He doesn't know what you are looking for, but the tone of your voice makes it quite clear that something exciting is going on. Surely it's more important than his momentary displeasure, and if he keeps up that racket he may never find out what the excitement is all about. So pretty soon he is looking too. If it's a bad day you may be very busy indeed, so it behooves you to get on with the lessons as quickly as possible—no baby cries underwater.

Everybody into the Pool

Your assistants will sit down next to each mother in turn. They will take the babies, holding them so that they cannot lose sight of their mothers, and wait until those mothers have slid into the water. (The mother should keep in mind that the baby has formed no opinion about the water in the pool. He didn't know anything about cod-liver oil either before someone put it in his mouth. It is the expression on the mother's face that gives the oil its taste and the pool its effect.) The baby is then passed with the minimum of space between into the mother's waiting arms.

Play

Move around among the bobbing, close-holding, talking group and introduce play. There really are people who don't know how to play with or talk to babies (or anyone else for that matter) because no one ever took the time to play with them or talk to them when they were little. Teasing, making funny faces, and even squirting water on an exposed tummy is fun. As long as the mother thinks these things are right and proper, the baby will too. Already she is setting the stage for his comparisons, attitudes, and prejudices.

Watch for the Chill

The babies will not be working very hard the first lesson or two and they may feel cold even in their mother's arms. Watch for the shiver or blue lips that signal a chill. That's the time to wrap the baby in the big towel, but don't take him away from the action. Let him watch the others from the sidelines. Babies love to watch and they learn by watching. Once the class advances to the kicking stage, then even the thin babies, who notice the cold more than fat babies, work harder and stay warm and comfortable.

Everybody out of the Pool

When it is time to leave, usually after a half-hour, establish a good-bye ritual that neither mothers nor babies can fail to recognize. Have the mothers make a large circle which brings them close to the rim of the pool. When they are all in place call out, "Ready to lift . . . one, two, three, *up*." It will be no time at all till *up* means *out*. Most babies know exactly what they can get away with, and that should be *nothing* in your swim class. You don't want half a dozen babies who aren't quite ready to leave kicking and screaming on their way to the locker room. It's bad for discipline.

Sometimes it's the mothers who are in need of discipline. It should be remembered that many young mothers of today were raised in yesterday's school of permissiveness. They were robbed of the opportunity to develop self-discipline by never being subjected to sensible parental discipline. The teachers who answered our questionnaire (see Appendix) had only one problem in their classes, the undisciplined mother of the undisciplined child. Set your rules

for both mother and child before anyone can put you in a position of having to handle a difficult situation.

Once the babies are in the up position, they are ready to go out. Without putting them back in the water the mothers should set them on the edge of the pool. At the first lesson the assistants can take the babies while the mothers clamber out. At the second lesson the mothers will learn the buddy system and be able to help each other.

Exercise

Most of the baby-swim classes incorporate baby exercises. One of the most successful of these classes is held at the YMCA in eastern Queens, New York. While the instructors freely admit that the swim part of the class is the "sell," the exercise is the most valuable. This was hard to get across at first, but more and more mothers are beginning to see the startling effect on their children. Eventually children who have learned to swim may drop out of swim classes, but they often go on with exercise classes which lead directly to tumbling, gymnastics, and dance.

In 1954 when the Institute for Physical Fitness reported to President Eisenhower that American children were very unfit, the failure rate for six-year-olds entering school was fifty-four percent. Today that figure has risen to over eighty percent. Failure to exercise babies properly during the early years has put children into a desperate state, but parents rarely are aware of this. You can tell them.

The exercises described in Chapter 4 are good for starters. If your mothers need a reason for the exercise part of your session, explain that the child who moves well will continue to keep active throughout life. In so doing, he will improve his circulation, improve his posture, and have the benefit of a strong relaxed body. He will also be able to concentrate better, retain more, and recall the information when he needs it, simply because he feeds more oxygen to his brain. And he will eat better, sleep better, and be easier to live with. A sluggish body fosters a sluggish mind and neither contributes to success. Failure begets moods and

even the will to fail. It is always better to be on the winning side.

If you can manage an exercise class in an adjoining room, you can start your tiny babies out on mats with their mothers helping them. Use music and demonstrate with one of the babies. Be sure to keep each exercise going long enough so that the mothers can pick it up and there is no confusion. When the babies reach the crawling stage you can begin tumbling with somersaults and wheelbarrows, which all little children love. Some simple gymnastic equipment will help. Babies who cannot even stand upright alone can climb ladders and swing sitting on a huge knot tied at the end of a rope. Babies who are just beginning to walk with help can do so with that same help on a balance beam.

If there is no other room available, you can do some exercises on the pool deck. Make them a part of the program —no exercise, no swim. The mothers will soon see what it is doing for their babies and may even be willing to provide it daily at home.

Showers

Babies love showers if they don't have to take them alone. They love to feel the warm water beating down on their backs. What's more, *you* are there, and you have smooth, sweet-smelling skin. With each different experience the boundaries of the baby's world are being pushed outward. He feels a little more, senses a little more, and knows a little more. Hold him close with his face away from the spray. Make sure the water is not too warm but warm enough to counteract the cold he may feel after coming out of the pool.

The Rubdown

Nobody ever fell off a floor, so put the baby down on it for his rubdown. It should be very thorough and should include lots of discussion and love. Above all, it should be a pleasant experience. For the baby a rubdown at the pool will be very different from the drying off after his bath at home. To begin with the sounds are different. Adults try to screen out extraneous sounds so that they can listen to words—they rarely listen just to sounds. Words mean nothing to babies, however, so they concentrate on sounds. No nursery has an echo and no nursery has ten or twenty other little babies also getting rubdowns after an exciting class.

Lasting Pleasure

The sounds, the lights, and the company will all contribute to your baby's conditioning. This is for the baby what a memorable experience in life is for you. If you were asked to call up some place that had pleasant memories, you would recall the sounds and the smells, what you were doing, and who was with you. If the baby's swimming experience is a success he will have a good feeling about similar surroundings even after he is grown up. He may not know why, but he will *like* going to the Y or the club. He will like the warmth and the echoing chatter of the locker room. He will feel comfortable there. He will like swimming and showers and rubdowns. In short, he will like doing what is good for his body and relaxing for his mind.

Your Turn

When the baby has had his swim, exercise, shower, and rubdown, he will probably be hungry. It is then that mommy should have a chance for a little swimming and water exercise herself. The buddy system will work well here. One mother can hold two baby bottles as easily as one, while her buddy goes back into the pool for either swimming laps or aqua exercises. The latter consists of walking or running through the water at the shallow end of the pool, jumping with feet apart and together, and kicking while holding onto the pool side. Almost any motion which uses the resistance of water to full advantage is good. These exercises are best done to music. If you swim laps, you will get better results in less time if you wear fins. If pool chemicals bother your eyes, wear a mask and snorkel. They are marvelous for spying on babies underwater as well. Once you have seen the way babies look underwater you will never be afraid for them again.

12
A STEP
AT A TIME

No two babies are alike. Some will take their lessons slowly, making slow and steady progress. Some will be ready for tomorrow yesterday. Still others go in little spurts. One day they are ready to learn three new things, and then for several weeks they remain right there without any advance. If all the babies are under four months, the age, according to Dr. McGraw, at which the swimming reflex seems to disintegrate, you should have instant swimmers. This is very rarely possible, however. The word "babies" can mean almost anything from eleven days old to a few weeks old to toddlers. Some baby-swim classes take any little person up to the age of three.

While age and sex do seem to make a difference in swimming progress, the real differences are presented by the mothers and teachers. That's where you come in. Once you have successfully taught a number of babies to swim, you will be an authority, even in your own eyes. Until that time you will be a little unsure. The lessons in this book go step by step—not necessarily week by week. One teacher will get her whole class propelling itself through the water at the first class on the first day, another may take ten lessons or more to get half the class going. That's a matter of presentation. One teacher will have trouble putting heart into the timid while another will allow herself to be browbeaten by one or more overweening mothers. That's personality. If you read this book carefully, you will know how a class can be run successfully. There are other ways, of course, but you won't discover them until you have taught for a while. Play it safe and follow directions just this first time.

Keep in mind that you are doing this work because you like it and you want to continue liking it. There *are* personalities, however, that cannot be either handled or endured. This is unfortunate, for if you tell such a person you cannot have her in class, the baby may lose his chance at many things, including your warm personality. If the mother is a class disrupter, you will have to find some means of separating her from the class. The disrupters are almost invariably the overambitious, and the logical solution for this type of woman is the private lesson. Offer it and set a good price on it. No one has any faith in a cheap article.

The Buddy System

Start the second class as you did the first, with the mothers sitting at the pool's edge holding their babies. This time no aides will be needed, because the mothers will learn to help each other. One mother holds two babies while the second slips into the water. Both babies are then passed to the mother in the pool who turns away from the mother on the edge, since we are still in the no-splash stage and want no startling experience to mar the input of the little computer.

Once again, start with close holding, bobbing, playing, and just looking. A baby spends an enormous amount of time looking, and such time is never wasted. Think what the baby in swim class sees that the baby at home in his nursery never sees. Patterns of light on the water, the shimmer of ripples on the tile wall, the lady with the gleaming hair and diamonds on her shoulders, the red ball bouncing in little waves, the drain that "talks." All of this is fascinating, and as you will soon discover, the baby keeps right on looking, even underwater.

Prone Position

Turn the baby tummy down in the water and hold him with both hands with his head up and his face toward you. This position presents a very different feel from close holding. Unless the baby is a "tub baby," he hasn't had the sensation of water against all of him at once. But while

he is free, he still has that wonderful sense of security flowing from the hands holding him. It would be the same for you if you were being supported by a pair of hands the size of a fork lift. And then, of course, there is always that smiling face.

Practice Makes Perfect

The rate at which you advance from one step to the next will also depend on the participation of the mothers. In the March 1962 issue of the *Physical Educator* there was an article entitled "Bathtub Babies," suggesting that mothers repeat the movements learned in the pool in the bathtub at home. This is the reverse of the method discussed in Chapter 5 and both work well. Suggest to your mothers that they practice your program at home. If you meet with resistance, remind them of the following: For a little while, your child will think you are just about all there is—surely till the age of six. That's about nine percent of his life if you figure his life expectancy as seventy. Six years later you will find that you have been reduced in stature, though not importance, by about half. During the next six years you probably will be relegated to out back somewhere, if not under the rug. When he is about midway through life, you may possibly emerge as a normal, fallible human being. You won't have a halo, but if he has gained any experience or wisdom, he will be able to see that you are in the same boat as he and may even be pulling a heavier oar. Don't wait for that day. Use the only time in your life you will ever be a goddess, and make it pay off. The student who gets most from school is the one who can come home and talk about what he learned with an interested parent. The swimmer, the musician, the rider, and the actor all appreciate an interested audience.

Do-It-Yourself Pool

If the mother has a basement or a heated garage you can even suggest installing a small portable pool for the practice sessions. A floor drain is helpful but not essential. Water can be put into the pool from the warm water faucet with a bit of rubber tubing. If there is no floor drain, it can be emptied with a siphon. The runoff for the water must be *slightly* lower than the bottom of the pool. If the basement floor is higher than the garden outside, run in a hose. First fill it with water, then put one end in the pool and one end out the window. As the outside end is lowered to the ground, the water in the hose will start to run out, pulling the pool water along with it. The pool will then be ready for clean water. If the basement is lower than the ground outside, build a platform for the pool and empty it with a siphon into a pail on the floor. To get this type of siphon going you use the same principle as that used to get gas out of a tank. Instead of filling a hose, you simply suck the water through the tube, and when you get a mouthful, pinch the tube closed until you have lowered it to the pail and then let it run.

Backyard Pool Seat

Working alone will present a problem that either a neighbor, a carpenter, or an auto supply store can remedy. It

will be a bit scary the first couple of times if the mother tries to carry the baby up a ladder and down a ladder. It also will be difficult to get into the pool while keeping the baby balanced on the edge. If a friend can hold the baby while the mother gets in and gets set, it will be easier. Failing that, a carpenter can build a little seat that can be hung over the edge—one the baby cannot fall from. Most auto supply stores carry kiddie seats that can be hung over both car seat and pool edge.

Whether your mothers use bathtub, backyard pool, or improvised setup in the basement, the results will be rewarding. Nothing quite takes the place of regular practice at home, and you will know which babies have had the benefit of such activity by their progress in the class.

13
MOVING
AHEAD

From this point on *movement* will be the key word, movement ahead in water. Pavlov conditioned dogs to salivate when a bell rang. Babies can be conditioned to kick their way along when they feel water passing over their skin as they move forward.

What the Skin Knows

To understand the full implication of this idea let's examine skin. Skin is made up of an outer layer, the epidermis, and an inner layer, the dermis, with a layer of subcutaneous tissue beneath. The epidermis has no blood vessels and, like hair and nails, no feeling. But just underneath that protective covering lies the dermis, which contains sweat glands, blood and lymph vessels, and millions of nerve endings. The slightest breeze passing over a mother's skin tells her where it touched her, the direction from which it came, and whether it was warm, hot, chill, cold, strong, mild, or a whisper. She gets all this information from long experience in feeling and making comparisons. The same breeze touching the baby's skin won't tell him anything except that there has been a change. While he does not lack the ability to feel that something has happened, he does lack *information* about breezes, so his little computer goes to work for him and does some input: (1) Something happened. (2) It happened while I was on my blanket on the floor without any clothes on. (3) It felt good. It will be some time before he can really say *why* he likes to be on his blanket without his clothes, but the minute he is stripped and placed there, he has a positive feeling about it. How many mothers will say with perfect assurance that her Johnnie or Jennie loves to lie on a blanket in the sun and kick? What makes her so sure? If she is a perceptive mother, she and Johnnie or Jennie have many ways of saying, "I like this."

With proper conditioning, those tiny nerves that lie just under the outer covering of the skin will begin to connect the feeling of moving forward through the water with kicking action. Your baby's skin is a veritable storehouse of information. Help him use it.

Tugging Away

When the baby makes his first move, the teacher acts as a mooring and the mother as a tug. It is you who holds him safe and close while the mother's hands are under his chest with palms up and thumbs curled over his shoulders. As she begins to step backward through the water, she pulls him away from his moorings and they are moving.

The water slides over all those millions of nerve endings and feels good. The fewer clothes the better it feels. That is why even grown-ups like to "skinny dip."

The really little babies, who still have their kicking reflex intact, will perform on cue, with face in the water. You will find that they can skip several intermediate steps and go right to work. The older children will have to be led into it a little more slowly, which is why it usually takes three lessons before most crying stops. If you make all this clear to the mothers *before* you start the class, you will make it easier for them, their babies, and yourself.

Kicking Up

Some babies kick two legs at once, some alternate legs, and some kick only one leg. There are a few who just lie stretched out and let both legs drag in the swirling water. It doesn't matter whether the baby is a one-leg kicker, a frog, or an aquaplane, his computer is taking it all in. Along with the swirl, the backward motion of the mother's body creates a suction which pulls the baby forward.

The form the kicking takes seems to depend on the baby's personality. Quiet babies kick less, and active babies more. This might tell us something about overactive, or hyperkinetic, children. According to The Joint Commission of Mental Health of Children, twenty-five percent of our children suffer from some emotional problem. Their symptoms vary widely. Some don't sleep well, some wake up screaming, still others have speech disorders, and a growing number fall into the category of hyperkinetic children. They can't sit still, they can't concentrate, they jiggle and jump, flap hands and arms, and interfere with

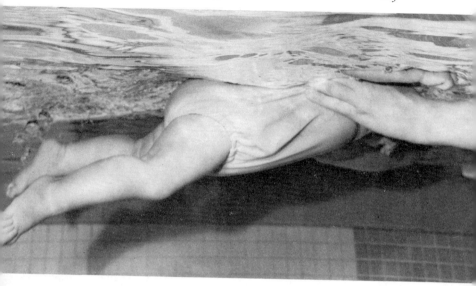

concentration and discipline of others. They are like cars idling at full throttle. One of the most disturbing aspects about their condition is the treatment they are often given. Instead of making sure that they get a full measure of physical activity commensurate with their obvious need to get rid of excess energies, they are given drugs to quiet them. The normal outlet for tension is action. Drugs mask the problem, they do not solve it.

A few years ago Elliot L. Richardson, then Secretary of Health, Education and Welfare, said that "behavior modifying drugs are not necessarily the best method of treating over-active school children." He added that "other effective treatment includes remedial education, family counselling and psychotherapy." More to the point, perhaps there is a way to *prevent* the development of such

problems when the first signs show up in babyhood. When a baby kicks superactively, he needs more of the same. He is telling you he needs an outlet. Give it to him. Superactive babies often turn out to be superbabies if given the chance to work off their excess energies. They can grow into superdifficulties, however, if they are penned up, stymied, and stopped from normal physical activity.

Teaching the Kick

If the baby is not a natural kicker, you can teach him. Pull him close to your chest, and with his head resting on your shoulder and his arms over yours, take the trailing legs in your hands and move backward. As you initiate the kicking motion, say the words, "Kick, kick, kick . . ." You will combine all the things the baby enjoys: closeness, praise, rhythmic and friendly noises, heartbeat—and forward motion.

Arm Motion

When kicking is achieved with some degree of regularity unassisted, the arms are freed. True arm action such as that used in the dog paddle comes when the child is older, but the use of arms to maintain stability comes quite early. Arms are to little babies what outriggers are to canoes, they keep the vessel from tipping over. Once the baby gets the feel of extended arms, he possesses stabilizing planes. He *feels* how they should be used, and uses them correctly. Imagine what a departure that is from the fetal position in which bent arms are held close to the sides.

To free the baby's arms the mother's hands should be

placed palms up under his chin, with the last two fingers giving support under the armpits. If the mothers will move backward in this position while the teacher from time to time stretches the baby's arms fully, the feel of a full stretch becomes part of the baby's movement vocabulary. There is something about water, probably its resistance, that makes stretching not only easy but pleasurable.

In this position swimming mothers can introduce a brand-new feel, that of being towed behind a swimmer. This is also an aid to keep the swimming mothers interested. Nonswimmers may be content to stroll around in the shallows, but good swimmers want to get at it and go swimming. It is just as important to build in challenge for the better athlete as it is to build in security for those who do not have water skills.

Circles

You can't work all the time. There has to be some fun time. Babies love the sensation of spinning in circles; it makes them dizzy. When they are older they will run out on the lawn on spring evenings or blustery fall days and turn in circles until they drop in a heap, whooping with laughter. Place your right hand under the baby's tummy and with your left grasp the arm nearest you. Start your turns to the right so he skids through the water planing on his chest, round and round in one direction until *you* are tired. Then change directions. This breaks up the lesson and gives both mother and baby a change of activity. After such a hilarious recess it is easy to go back to work again.

Swizzles

Another playtime activity is *swizzles*. Hold the baby under the arms and lift him out of the water so that just his legs are submerged. Drag him left and right through the water with as much speed as you can muster. Speed appeals to children if it's controlled. Keep in mind that they don't go to the movies, watch TV, or read books. They get their kicks from *feeling*, and the greater the variety of feelings, the greater their sense of awareness. That is a quality that can be instilled, educated, and retained. How aware are you? Who is the most aware person you know? Who is the least? What would you consider the advantages of being an aware person?

Pass the Baby

There is still another game all children love called *pass the baby*. It involves the excitement of moving through space from one pair of safe, loving hands to another. The best pairs of persons are those who love the baby. While parents are eminently suited for the game, grandmothers often qualify.

Today's grandmother may be as young as her mid thirties or well past her fifties. Age is not a primary consideration, but there are ways of determining how a grandmother will take to the idea of a swimming grandchild. If she was an athlete, a dancer, or a tomboy in her youth, she'll take to it fine. If she was not so physically active, she may lack

confidence, but that doesn't mean keep her out of the water. Who knows, today's nervous granny may turn out to be tomorrow's very effective assistant. Give her a chance, but be gentle.

Take the time to explain what you are doing and why.

Pass the baby into the grandmother's waiting hands several times before turning the mother-grandmother team loose on their own. When you feel the grandmother is relaxed (and not before) have the mother and grandmother face each other over a gap of about ten feet of water. The baby starts out in the mother's arms and *you* move the baby across the gap to the waiting hands of the grandmother. After two trips from one to the other, they can proceed on their own. At that point they draw close enough so that they can pass the baby to each other from hands to hands. This is excellent preparation for *pass the baby under*, an underwater exercise discussed on page 169. During this lead-up activity the baby gets used to going from one person to another, being loved and praised at each terminal, and always finding someone home when he gets there.

14
FLOATING FREE

Learning to float is very important, particularly for a baby. It is the most valuable trick he will carry in his little bag of skills should he ever find himself up to his neck or over his head in water. All it takes is familiarity with the medium—and "inner water wings."

Vital Capacity

One of the prerequisites of a good back float is a good *vital capacity*. This refers to the maximum amount of air that can be taken into the lungs with one inhalation. Dancers, runners, swimmers, singers, and, believe it or not, the colicky baby all have good vital capacity. Their particular interests (and in the baby's case, problem) require lots of air and the more they exercise their lungs, the greater their capacity. (Anyone suffering through three months of colic with its accompaniment of howls, yowls, and screams knows what good vital capacity is all about.)

Lungs might be thought of as inner water wings. If you put on a pair of fully inflated water wings and try to sink, you will fail. If you take a really full breath of air and you have reasonably good vital capacity, you will not sink. Even those people with large bones, well-developed muscles, and little fat will remain buoyant if they have developed their lungs. They may not be as effective as those of the lightweight and bouncy butterball who does not require much support, but they will make the difference between peril and safety.

You can test your vital capacity and that of children old enough to follow directions with a tape measure. Measure the circumference of your chest with lungs empty and again when your lungs are full. The difference in the two measurements give you, in inches, your vital capacity. A singer or climber, runner or swimmer may measure as much as four inches, a sedentary child as little as one-half inch. There are some people who can press out their ribs to get a better score than their lung capacity entitles them to, but that is no reason for discarding the tape measure method. The object for everyone is to improve. Running improves vital capacity, so run. Get the children running too. A child of three can run a mile a day with no strain at all. You and they will develop water wings that cannot be left at the beach.

The Back Float

Begin your class with the usual cuddle and bob activities and then select a baby from the group for demonstration. Ask the mothers to lend you a baby who likes to sleep on his back. From a close-hold position, extend your arms slightly, which puts him on his back just a little way from your chest. You will be able to give good support at both bottom and upper back and at the same time be able to lean over the little head you want to lie back in the water. There should be lots of conversation and smiling going on. This tells the baby that although this angle may feel different, the safety and companionship are the same.

Keep the mothers close together as they copy you. This builds a feeling of group safety and participation. It is quite true that babies are completely self-centered. They won't share their toys and everything centers around their needs and wants, but they do feel the presence of others. They also feel the air of fun and excitement and they react to it with pleasure. If one baby does send up a wail of protest, the others will usually ignore it. After all, what is one voice of protest in a sea of contentment?

With the babies on their backs, do some group milling, with the mothers moving close together. This serves as reinforcement and also fosters group thinking, which can have a powerful and positive effect. The sharing of good things is a very human need. If two people are sharing pleasant thoughts and activities it doubles the magic. If a whole group is sharing them, the enjoyment is multiplied many times. Both the mothers and the babies feel it. They can't put a name to it, but those who partake of it will be back next week and the week after.

The Lineup

Until now you have used group milling for that feeling of security everyone needs at the start. Now, to avoid collisions, have the mothers line up in the center of the pool.

As we saw in our discussion of the tub float, most babies placed on their backs, in or out of water, will curl their legs into the fetal position. When the legs are not supported by water, however, they weigh a great deal, and both head and torso go under. Babies don't respond to the warning, "Straighten your legs or you'll sink." You have to give their bodies a reason to straighten the legs. The procedure is essentially the same as that used in the tub. If the babies are thrust feet first out in front of their mothers their immediate worry is "Where is she?" A quick look around locates her right behind his head. But there's only one way to maintain that nice safe feeling—keep looking. When babies turn their eyes upward for even a few minutes their eyes become tired. If, however, the head is tilted back, a baby can keep the mother in view indefinitely. The head that is resting back in the water is much more floatable than the one that is held aloft with eyes looking at toes. And with the head back it's easier to stretch legs.

Contact

At your signal the mothers start walking backward pulling the babies along. The straight line prevents crashes that would take the mother's attention away from the baby. Maintenance of that connection is highly important. True contact with another human being, even one's own child, is more rare than you might suspect. The success of a mother-baby relationship, with emotional stability and adjustment, is due more to the closeness and completeness of the contact than to the length of time spent in each other's company. It is quite possible to be physically near

another person yet miles apart in thought and in what is sometimes called soul.

Many parents bathe, dress, feed, change, and move their babies about without ever making true contact. Their minds are too busy elsewhere. All minds wander sometimes, but when a parent's mind wanders all the time, it may be depriving the baby emotionally during the most important time of life—the pattern-setting, attitude-forming beginnings. Keep drumming into your group that it is the contact that counts. The smiles must *mean* something. The words must convey *feeling*, the hugs must *speak*, and the mind must *communicate* something, something the baby

needs to know with every cell in his body—that he is truly loved.

Lying on his back with two strong hands under him, the baby feels very secure indeed, and even a new face does not upset his equanimity. So again, borrow one of the babies and proceed with your demonstration. With your arms holding him securely on both sides, reach down and grasp the baby's legs at the knees so they can be straightened. As you walk backward through the water moving his legs to kick up a good-sized wake, the baby gets a message. The feeling is different yet somehow familiar, and the computer registers another sensation.

It is not necessary to be rich to be advantaged, just as it is not necessary to be poor to be deprived. These swimming babies are advantaged in ways the house-bound baby will never know. Their mothers may not be able to spend more than a little time with them each day, but think of the wealth of sensation they are sharing through eyes, ears, mouth, fingers—and skin.

15
SUBMARINES ALL

If you have tiny babies in your class, some of them undoubtedly will go underwater with their mothers in the first few days. But if you have a wide age spread you may have to wait for "submarine day." You prepare for this event by talking about it well in advance, not for the baby's sake, but so the mother will be ready. The teacher who works alone with one baby at a time knows when she is ready to take the baby under, and the baby takes his cue from her. In a class, the mothers determine the reactions of their babies, so make it important, and work for expectancy.

Make It Special

It is difficult to think of two things at the same time or entertain two emotions at the same time, even when we say we have "mixed emotions." The emotion you don't want the mother to have is anxiety, so you edge out anxiety and ease in expectancy. Here are some ways to make the day special.

Submarines are often named for fish. Each of your babies might be given a little certificate bearing the date of the dive, the baby's name, and the fish name he has earned. There should also be a line bearing his mother's name as coach. If the date and circumstances surrounding the appearance of a first tooth are important, how much more important to the baby's record should be his first dive underwater.

Successful dives can be rewarded with little plastic fish to take home to show daddy, the grandparents, or the bridge club. Whatever the prizes, have them in full view with whatever other little decorations you can manage. It isn't the baby you are trying to please and excite, it's the mother. You are building expectancy.

Going Under

Line the mothers up on the edge as you did the first day and remind them again of the following:

1. Their babies were in water for nine months.
2. They are used to being held close and they like it.
3. Young babies do not have to be taught to hold their breath, they come into the world with that reflex.

Start with the usual ritual of close holding, cuddling, bobbing, smiling, and friendly noises. This time, however, the cuddling has a new form. The baby is held close with his head pressed against your neck so that as you sink, the water does not rush up his nose but flows in a swirl along your body. The arm pressing the head close runs all the way up the back. You come as close to a womblike sur-

rounding for the child as you can. Be sure his face is under your chin.

Next, even though the baby doesn't understand one word, tell him distinctly that you and he are going under the water to look around. Prepare for your dunk by saying clearly and cheerfully, "Here we go, one, two, three, *down*." As you say the word "down," sink down under the water. Don't jump up in the air first, simply bend your knees and sink. There is no need to go deep, just be sure your head (and the baby's) goes beneath the surface. Important note: Don't shove the baby under while you stay on top to keep your hair dry for the PTA meeting. That's like sending a child to Sunday school while you lie snug in bed. It won't take. You go down together so that all the surfaces of your bodies remain in contact. You want the closeness and the water all around him to remind him of that nice "other place."

Don't Stop Halfway

Be sure you go all the way down in one dunk. If you stop at eye level the baby will be forced to make a decision, breathe or not breathe. The chances are good that he will choose wrong.

You will note in the photograph on the following page several things.

1. The baby is very young, just a few weeks old.
2. The mother is calm and therefore the baby is too.
3. There was hardly a ripple when they sank.
4. No two people could be closer together.

When you reach full squat don't gather for a great rush back up. Even without any practice adults can hold their

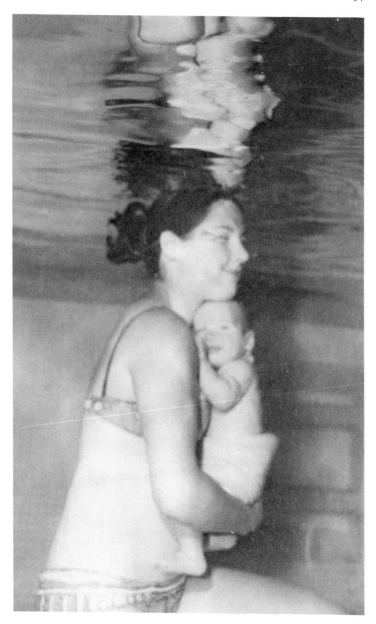

breath for quite a long time. Young babies can hold theirs much longer with no discomfort at all and certainly no wish to breathe while under. The first dive should take at least three seconds *after* you are on the bottom. Count three seconds this way: "One-chim-pan-zee, two-chim-pan-zees, three-chim-pan-zees," then surface *slowly* making no splash at all. It is noise and confusion that scare babies, not being underwater.

A Pat on the Back

If your baby does misjudge his environment (and the chances are in direct proportion to the length of time he

has been out of the womb), he will cough, splutter, and wail. Pat him on the back and raise one or both arms in the air. Tell him, even if he can't understand your words, that he took a breath too soon. He will get over his distress quickly, and before he has a chance to connect *dunk* with *splutter*, go down again.

One teacher in Oregon who has taught hundreds of babies to swim has never had a baby cough or splutter. However, she has taught all those babies herself and never let a mother do the job. Mothers may not be experts with their first babies, but they can learn and they offer the advantage of a high teacher-student ratio—just about one per baby.

When the mothers dive in a group they lend each other courage, and when you go down with them they feel still better. If three out of four babies surface without incident, the one snorter is very much in the minority and doesn't seem tragic even to his mother.

Ready or Not

Give the successful divers about a minute of bob-cuddle-smile-praise and make ready to dunk again. The snorter may take a little longer to gather his forces but as soon as the noise drops to a whimper, down he should go. There is a system of crash teaching for little children being used today in which they are taken under over and over, ready or not. This may seem like the cruelest kind of forcing, but it works. Children soon learn that yelling underwater does no good, taking a big breath and holding it while underwater, on the other hand, works. There isn't time to yell between dunks, so might as well close mouth, hold breath, and be comfortable. Babies learn fast.

Stay with It

Of course the deciding factor in this situation (as in every one you will encounter) is the mother. There are some babies who protest everything and always will. Hopefully, the child with a resisting nature will have a mother with the same kind. One little boy was brought to exercise class at the Institute for Physical Fitness for six solid sessions, and for six solid sessions he sat in a corner and wouldn't even take his shoes off. His mother gave up sitting with him after the third, but didn't give up bringing him—and that was the secret. He had nobody to show off for or to resist. His determination wavered at the seventh class when somersaults were being taught. He announced that he could do a better one than the demonstrator, and proceeded to prove it. From that moment on he missed no classes and stayed with us until he graduated from high school. He

went on to college with a football scholarship. Think what he would have missed if his mother hadn't been as obstinate as he was.

If one child continues to complain, send the mother to the showers and you or an aide take over the baby for a couple of weeks. The bright mother will go willingly but there are some who cannot bear to demand anything of a child nor to hear him cry. She may think she runs the child but it's the other way round. Such a mother will drop out early in the game and you are the better off for it. Do not refund the tuition. That baby filled a place another baby could have filled. If *you* have to ask that mother to withdraw, then you should refund—and you still will be better off.

Masks

If you can manage to have some skin-diving masks available for mothers to wear either during the dunk or for watching while you dunk the babies, they will get over their worries at once. All they will see down there are perfectly happy little water people.

After a few weeks of dunking, the mothers will be able to go down singly or in groups and simply *sit* on the bottom. As they become more at ease, urge them to open their eyes and look around them. Their faces soon become as relaxed as their babies' and little by little they can increase the length of the dunk.

16
FATHER'S DAY

When a new baby comes into the home there is great rejoicing and there are many changes. Life for the young parents will never be quite the same again. The mother's role changes dramatically, and she is busy every hour of the day and part of the night with her new charge. Caring for a little life is exciting and fun—and time-consuming. While she is aware of her singular responsibility, the father may be aware of something quite different, a feeling that his place as number one has been usurped. It hasn't really, but for a while he may feel acutely uncomfortable and then acutely guilty because of this discomfort. You can remedy this situation by making him a participant as soon as possible.

The Masculine Touch

In a society that takes most fathers away from home much of each day any contact with a man is very pleasant and helpful for a baby who is filing away impressions. The YMCA in Leominster, Massachusetts, is particularly for-

tunate. It is near an army base, where a program called
Operation Transition has been set up to help prepare young
soldiers for civilian life. Many sign up for Y work as part
of the program and the baby-swim classes are very popular.
Most of the men are highly enthusiastic and want to get
right into the pool and work with the babies, not next
week, not when they get back to Kalamazoo or Denver,
but right away.

Boy babies especially need men around them, since the majority of their teachers during the important years are likely to be women. Girl babies need men around them more often too. They are born flirts and seem to love mustaches. An upset baby usually quiets down at once when taken over by a man. Perhaps that is because only the man who delights in babies volunteers to help with them and that feeling is transmitted to the baby.

Some groups run baby-swim classes on Sundays so that the whole family can attend, and many Ys provide family nights, which give daddy a chance to get into the swim.

Showing off for Daddy

Fathers often don't know how important they are. Even if you can't get them into the pool the first time, the mere fact that they are there lends fins to their children. The man may not have known what his child could do before he came to a swim class, and what's more, his child may not have known. Showing off for daddy can put a child weeks ahead in self-confidence.

A crying baby doesn't say the same things to his father, or to any man for that matter, as he says to his mother.

The mother hears all those pitiful words, the man hears the noise. Men can tell when there is real distress, but they are not so perturbed by noise, and babies often give up in disgust at the apparent lack of linguistic skill. The day the fathers come to class urge them to take the submarines down. If they feel their swimmers have been trained they'll be only too happy to cooperate. It will be good for both them and the babies, and it may turn out to be the first of a series of family swims.

Keep Them Together

Just as mothers are often isolated when they have little ones to care for, young fathers often give up going down to the Y or club for exercise, a game of squash, or handball. Parenthood can be a blessing or a trap, depending on what you make of it. You would be doing many parents a favor if you could arrange for a quiet room somewhere so that after the swim all those babies could take a snooze while the parents spend some time and have some fun together. The step from single to married is often made when people

are very young. The next step, from a fancy-free existence to one of responsibility and financial strictures, may
be close behind. Baby-sitters are expensive unless such a
luxury can be shared with several others. As long as you
are doing so much for so many already with your swim
classes, you might as well go ahead and strengthen a few
marriages.

17

BABIES
AND SEALS

You might ask why babies seem so totally unconcerned in the face of asphyxiation. A look at some aquatic mammals may provide an answer. It is logical to assume that the dolphins and seals, which can stay underwater for long periods (as long as six minutes for the dolphin and up to an hour for some species of seal), must have some special protective device. Their brain, like man's, suffers death if not provided with oxygen and glucose. An extraordinary vital capacity, which might provide great quantities of stored air, could not be the answer, since any animal depending on such a reserve would have to be all lung. There must be another explanation.

Studies conducted by Dr. Robert Elsner and his associates at the Scripps Institute of Oceanography in La Jolla, California, have shed some light on this interesting phenomenon. They have shown that when animals are underwater, they do not consume as much oxygen as when they have free access to air. In a number of tests on seals and dolphins, Dr. Elsner found that the heart, which pumps blood to all parts of the body, slows down as soon as the

animal's face is submerged. In the case of dolphins, the heart often slows down even before immersion, as soon as the target of their diving stunt comes into view.

The Diving Response

In seals the heartbeat can drop from one hundred to eight beats a minute. This would seem to make survival precarious, but here a second metabolic change comes into play. At the instant of diving there is a complete rerouting of the blood flow away from those parts of the body less vulnerable to oxygen starvation—the flippers, kidneys, and digestive organs, for example. With these areas effectively isolated, the available oxygen is directed to the two most vulnerable centers, the heart and the brain. (Nature has taken care to protect unborn babies of mammals who dive in search of food, however. While the blood supply to most of the mother's body is reduced during submersion, the blood supply to the fetus remains constant.)

Are Men Like Seals?

Does man have a similar advantage? To some extent he does. While tests are incomplete and none have been done on babies to date, there are indications that man's heart, too, slows down when he is submerged. The rate varies with each individual and is not as great in the old as in the young, but there is one example of a man who was immersed for only thirty seconds and lowered his heartbeat from the normal seventy-two beats a minute to thirteen. And as the arteries in a seal's flippers close off the blood flow to a mere trickle during a dive, so the blood flow to a man's extremities is reduced during submersion.

Teach a Seal to Swim?

Few people realize that seals, like humans, must be taught to swim. The baby seal on the next page, separated from his mother, is six months old and is just learning to swim by having his head dunked in a basin. (Submersion of the head is really the most important factor in learning to swim.) Under ordinary circumstances, this seal would have been land bound for only a month, at which time his mother would have stopped nursing him and taught him to dive for food. A baby seal is a pretty poor swimmer at first, but hunger is a quick teacher. Soon he can stay underwater from one to four minutes. By the time he is four or five months old his diving response has developed

to the point where he can stay down a full fifteen minutes, and when he is a year old he is the equal of an adult.

Might not the human's diving response also improve if developed early and used more or less continuously? And if so, what practical value would it have? Keep in mind the following points:

1. Immersion can slow the heartbeat drastically.
2. Under these circumstances, the blood flow is routed to critical organs, the heart and brain.
3. A body that can thus adapt to the hostile environment of water can widen the margin of time between immersion and asphyxiation.

The seal dives that he may live. Could not man dive to improve his survival mechanism so that he might live better, safer, and longer? Of course, swimming for the adult learner may always be a little foreign. But swimming for the baby, who began life in a water environment, is a part of his being.

18
DIVE! DIVE! DIVE!

Being held close and submerged soon has its graduation day. The baby is then ready for the next step, a headfirst dive. Until "dive day," going underwater is a shared experience between the mother and the baby, but now the mother begins to move away so that the baby will learn to depend on himself. All babies are water-safe when held in their mother's arms. It is when those arms are not there that the baby has to know what to do.

Pushover

Remind the mothers again that the babies are comfortable underwater. If you have provided diving masks, the mothers will see it for themselves. By this time the baby has been conditioned to kick as water slides by, sending his body forward. Now you want to teach the baby to find where up is and how to get there—and why he ought to bother. Place your left hand under the baby's chest and your right at the back of his head and neck. The baby has heard "Here we go, one, two, three, *down*" often

enough to be fully warned. To him those words and tone mean, "Hold your breath, we're going under." By this time it won't matter if you hold him close in your arms, by his legs or by one ear, he's still going to hold his breath. You have already given him a basic protection against one of the major causes of drowning, panic.

Keeping your left hand steady, push the head downward and forward. Take two steps forward and then bring his head to the surface. What will he see as he comes up to you? Smiles and laughter, praise and hugs. He has every reason to find out how to come up. You are there. Love is just about the strongest motivation there is. Now he not only can kick himself forward in the water but he knows where to find you.

After you have practiced this over and over successfully and have built confidence, you move on to the next step. Grasp the shoulder nearest you in your right hand and place the left under the lower abdomen. Holding the baby's head just above the surface, raise his lower body high and drop him gently into the water, keeping hold of his right shoulder as he goes down. Be sure to lift the lower body high enough so that he goes in head first and not face first. After he has learned a little about propelling himself underwater, you will be able to let go of the controlling arm and he will pop to the surface on his own power.

To get his head out of the water when he is prone, a baby must lift it, and very few little babies can do that. However, if a baby is underwater and kicking his way to the surface he will come up in an upright position, not horizontally. His head will emerge naturally, just as yours would if you pushed up to the surface. He too can take a deep breath, and he will. In their early years, many

young swimmers spend their time playing around under-water, pushing to the top when in need of air, then diving again. They are like young dolphins, to whom water is just like home.

Travel

Travel is just an extension of the *pushover*. Again we must be more concerned with the mother than with the baby. She may understand that babies can normally stay under longer than adults, but elapsed time is hard to judge when her "pride and joy" is being shoved along under-water while she is breathing air. The mother doesn't know how the baby feels, she only imagines how *she* would feel. She cannot see the delighted little face; she can only see the back of a sleek head and feel the struggling little body as it churns along just below the surface. This is mask time again.

Incidentally, there *are* people who feel claustrophobic in a mask. Lend them one with a snorkel and tell them to sit in a chair and watch one commercial on TV without re-moving it. Next they should do a little housework with it on and then a little exercise. When they return to the pool have them sit with the mask, submerged, for five sec-onds in the shallow end and gradually increase the time. Bring the baby by, face immersed, as they sit and watch. They will soon be able to manage it quite well and you will have given the whole family a gift. The mother who wants to go skin diving takes *everybody* along.

At this point the ambitious mothers will need as much attention as the timid mothers previously have needed. These mothers feel they should push their children. But

just as there are children who need a little pushing from time to time, there are others who should never be pushed. They'll get there, but in their own time. Nature does not always see fit to team mothers with babies of similar temperaments. As underwater travel progresses the babies cover longer and longer distances, but there are limits to the distances that individual babies want to go. Try to pay as much attention to the overconscientious pusher as to the mother who keeps pulling the baby up to see if he's still all right.

Start the baby with the pushover dive, and when he is about a foot beneath the surface, travel him forward. If he fails to kick and just seems to be going along for a ride, don't fret. He is enjoying it. He likes the feel of the water against his face and along his sides, arms, and legs. As you work with his kick on the surface he will get the idea.

Drinking Can Be a Problem

Some babies do drink the pool water. In fact they often drink quite a lot of pool water. It's the first time they've ever had free access to all the water they could drink. Don't worry about the chemicals, they are probably getting more in their canned baby food.

There is one small problem, however, which is easily handled. When they imbibe too freely their stomachs fill up and they become uncomfortable. They are not capable of tying cause (drinking pool water) to effect (stomach discomfort). They do, however, often mix up cause and effect. You don't want two bits of information in the baby's computer to overlap, *stomach ache—swimming*. That could ruin everything. Before discomfort reaches a boil (you can

tell by checking the size of his abdomen; if it's distended, he's been drinking), press your hand gently against the bulge and the water will return to the pool. It's no trick at all for a baby to spit up the water he has just swallowed —and it comes up unattended by his last meal.

19
HONING
THE SKILLS

The baby now knows how to kick and is familiar with both forward movement and holding his breath under water. With the added security of knowing that the hand on his head or the back of his neck belongs to a friend, he is ready to develop his skills still further.

Remote Control

Travel was done with the mothers moving along next to their babies. *Remote control* is accomplished with the mothers in front of their babies. Place the baby in the prone position with his head in the water. Hold his entire head in firm but gentle hands and start to move backward at a fairly good speed so that the water provides suction as it swirls from you. As soon as you have momentum and the baby is kicking, change your hold from two hands to one. Place your fingers at the back of the baby's head just where it curves into the neck and draw him along in a series of light taps. Go only a couple of feet at the start.

Remind the mothers that they are not training the babies for a team at this point, but are simply conditioning them to kick hard enough to stay with them as they move backward. Then fingers become merely aids which will be withdrawn as soon as the idea has been firmly established.

Be sure to watch your mother-baby pairs at work. Encourage the timid and even take over for them the first few times, keeping the baby moving a little longer than the mother might. Suggest to the overambitious mother that a shorter run will consolidate the baby's gains and make for greater progress in the end. After a few more lessons there will be less and less need for even finger contact once the baby has been placed face down in the water and given the initial pull. The baby will be aware that his mother is there in front of him, and the bright colors of her suit will mark the direction he is to go. In time he will swim equally well to reach a toy or the edge of the pool or the shore. When that happens *you* get the medal!

Pass the Baby Under

When the baby has become accustomed to the *pushover, travel,* and *remote control,* he is ready to play *pass the baby under.* At first the passer pushes the baby directly

into the catcher's hands so that the baby does not travel alone. Start with a couple of surface passes, then a push-over with travel, and then the underwater pass.

In the beginning there may be a tendency to grab what-ever comes forward first, a hand or occasionally the head.

Good catching comes with practice just as does good passing. When the passer and catcher are sure of their team-
work step back a little and begin to pass through a little
space. With each successful pass step back a little more to
increase the distance between pairs of hands.

The deeper the pass, the more time the baby will have for his underwater crossing without his natural buoyancy bringing him to the surface. Stand far enough apart so that depth of pass, force of pass, and distance of pass all

work together. If you stand too far apart at first and if the baby has not been started deep enough or if the push was weak, he may surface before he reaches the catcher's hands. You want him to be able to surface on his own, but you want to choose the time.

The baby already knows the difference between swimming underwater and on the surface. The area of uncertainty is that tiny margin in between. Until he is conditioned to breathe not only when his *eyes* are out of water but when his *mouth* is out, there may be some confusion, with accompanying sounds of distress. Very little babies like to be turned upside down and "emptied" upon arrival. That is what the doctor is doing when he hangs the neonate by his heels. There is a very important difference, however. Here the baby is supported close to another body, which must make him feel very safe indeed—note the expression on the baby's face in the photograph. Waterdrops don't bother his eyes any more than water hinders his looking around when he is under it. Fear of water in the eyes only comes to children who start swimming lessons when they are older. Notice something else, too, the gentle-

ness of the man's hands both as he receives and as he lifts the child. There is no tension in those hands, nor are his nails long and scratchy.

Free Travel Underwater

In this lesson the pass is made as before, but deeper. The strength of the push should carry the baby to a few feet within reach of the catcher before he starts to surface. If the pass is straight the baby's extended arms will keep him stable and on course. Instead of catching with both hands and lifting the baby out of the water, the catcher puts her fingers on the back of the baby's head and pulls him

forward *at the deeper level* as she moves backward. This works the same way as does *remote control* on page 167.

Strong forward motion is what you are working for. A person swimming underwater can stay at the desired depth merely by moving forward with enough speed to keep the water flowing over his body. His torso and his arms act like the fuselage and wings of a plane. The air flows from the leading edges of a plane's wings and lifts or lowers the plane according to the angle. If there is not enough speed

to the forward motion of the plane it stalls out and falls. If the baby loses momentum underwater he too stalls out. If this happens and he does not have his arms in the proper position, he loses stability and rolls over. His computer and his sinuses tell him that is not the right position and he becomes confused. When he is older he will know enough to kick hard and regain his speed or he will know how to adjust his arms to bring about stability. He may even do one or the other or both now because of his conditioning, but try to avoid the confusion by providing a firm thrust and a stable send-off. In between passes take time out to visit with other resting babies. Play with a few toys, listen to the "talking" drain. The baby quickly forgets what he was doing in the excitement of the new, and when you go back to work again, work is again new.

As the pass is repeated, the passer and catcher move further and further apart so that the baby must travel longer distances unaided. Remember, the baby *sees* where he is going and his kick is getting stronger and fuller.

No action the baby can institute out of water works on his legs, feet, and ankles as the swimming kick does. Note how much his feet resemble fins. The kick also strengthens thigh muscles. This is particularly important today. In an earlier era when children normally walked long distances to school, the thigh muscles were developed in the process. Now most children do not strengthen those muscles very much and that in turn means weak knees.

Also, no other activity can make a baby stretch out as swimming does. In unexercised babies the fetal position persists for a long time. The swimming baby is working hard and well on both strength and flexibility, and it is these two qualities which produce coordination.

Certainly, swimming should be a basic for overweight babies. Fat babies are slow to move and since they are slow, their fat stays with them. The thin wiry babies are off and crawling—and later off and running—to see what's over there. Their horizons widen with every passing hour. The fat baby sits and looks and by the time he has enough muscle to move his bulk around, what was over there is gone. This unhealthy, unhappy state continues all through childhood and by the time the parents become aware that a problem exists, another has been added. Soon he is no longer just a chubby baby or a fat little kid, he's a sad and frustrated human being and he's not likely to recover. So swim, baby, swim. A good exercise program will help too, but in the water the fat baby can help himself.

20
UNDERWATER PLAY

Circles and *swizzles* are surface games. The games that follow are underwater games. If the mother is not proficient enough to play with her baby underwater, try to arrange for some visiting playmates once in a while. The ideal playmate swims well and likes babies. Those requirements exclude no age group or sex. A granny may swim like a fish, as do many teens. Men are just as good as women, and one certainly need not be a parent to qualify.

Rendezvous

The passer takes the baby under, and the catcher is already there waiting for the exchange to take place. Whoever heard of hugging underwater? This baby did.

The baby is then passed to the waiting catcher but instead of surfacing immediately, they turn and travel a little distance together. This reinforces the idea that it is possible to swim forward underwater as well as just go back up again and readies the baby for *hoop play* (page 194).

Hand in Hand

For a little while do something that every baby does every day and all day long. Look at the hands of people you know well. Note all the ways those hands advertise what that person is thinking and feeling. Can you imagine anger without a fist? Grief without a wringing of hands? Kindness without a reassuring pat? Or love without a caress?

Did you know you can consciously direct what you are feeling to your hands and because of it the feeling will be stronger? Make an experiment. Sit just as you are and look at the picture of the baby girl on this page. Imagine that you are waiting for her underwater and that in just a few seconds she will swim into your hands.

Let your hands rest in your lap while you "think" a welcome into every part of them. Almost immediately you

will feel it. The feeling will start in the fingers and you will have an urge to open your hands wide. They will feel a little heavier as though something was there that had not been there a second before. Then you will feel something in your thumbs. They will want to open as if to make room for the tiny body swimming toward you. Both hands will feel somehow full, open, and ready. This would happen spontaneously if you actually reached out to catch the baby, but not nearly to the degree it happens when you really prepare for it through concentration.

Note carefully both the passer's and the catcher's hands as the baby pictured here moves from one set to the other. They are lightly but firmly held and while you can *see* the absolute delight in the catcher's face, the baby *feels* it.

Babies also enjoy being thrust through the water by the powerful kick of a good swimmer. Sometimes the feel of

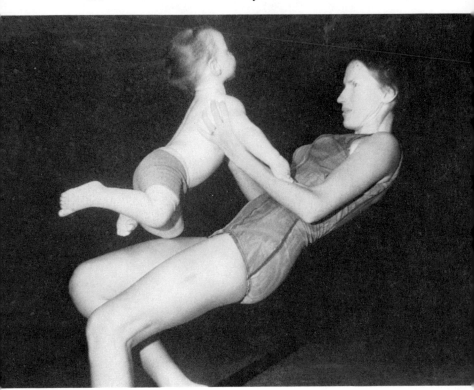

the water flowing past so quickly moves them to kick with a pretty good power themselves, so it is wise to hold them far enough out in front to prevent a belt to the solar plexus.

Piggyback

All babies like to ride piggyback on land and it's no different in the water. When you start this game you will have

to hold their hands close to the straps on your shoulders. Men who have no such straps can loop some sash cord (any material with body will do) over their shoulders like bandoliers. If the baby has been regularly exercised with his fingers grasping the fingers of his "coach" (page 27) for several months, he not only has his original reflex grip, but a well-developed strength as well. Once he gets the idea

that he is supposed to hold onto those straps, he will. You can hurry this procedure by playing piggyback at home and teaching him to hold straps rather than neck. Do this by supporting his seat and leaning forward a bit after his hands have been closed around your straps.

When the strap hold has been learned and is fairly reliable you can swim down into the deeper water with the baby, always remembering that the baby is not the least bit worried. He has no word for shallow or deep. He just knows he's in the water. When you take the baby down with you, don't try to surface dive as you would if you were alone. Just sink and then start forward and down like a submarine sliding under the surface.

When you reach the bottom, your rider may elect to release his hold and take off on his own. You can either head him toward the surface by shoving upward with your back or by turning around and pushing with your hands. With time and practice the baby will start kicking his way up as soon as he releases his hold.

21
WATER
TOYS

Imagine a world without flowers and trees, a world like the moon. What do you suppose little moon babies would play with? Now imagine a coral reef in the Caribbean with its wild display of color, its coral and floral gems, and its glittering tropical fish. The plain tile floor of a pool is pretty empty unless you fill it with treasures. But what is treasure for a baby? It is color and shape and feel: something that wasn't there yesterday; something to grasp and then put in the mouth. Water toys like bathtub ducks and boats, shiny rubber balls, bouncing balloons, even empty bleach bottles are fine for on the surface, but what about under the water? Any brightly colored object that will sink to the bottom and is small enough to grasp but too big to swallow will do. It will be new and exciting to him.

Hidden Treasure

The baby likes variety, so in between swimming lessons do a little treasure hunting. Later, when he is older, he will love going down and looking around in almost any water.

He may never know when his insatiable curiosity was born, but he will be happy to have it. That's the kind of curiosity that makes skin and scuba diving so fascinating. So teach him that there is treasure at the bottom of the sea.

Hoop Play

Another way to lend variety to lessons is to present the challenge of a passage to go through. Plastic hoops can be anchored at any depth with two lengths of string tied about a foot apart. Fishing weights make good anchors and so do little socks filled with pebbles.

Begin the introduction to *hoop play* with the familiar underwater pass. It may be a little while before the baby takes in the fact that there is more to this kind of pass—there's something colorful to pass through.

If the hoop is big enough, you can swim through *with* the baby. If the hoop is too small and you don't have a passer handy, you can take the baby down and push him through with one hand from the side. This gives you ample

time to get to the surface ahead of him so you can greet him upon arrival. For the present, you want to be sure someone is waiting to catch him. Later, when you are teaching him to swim to the edge of the pool, you will be

able to set the hoop close enough to the edge so he will surface a few feet away. A gentle push in the right direction will soon convey the idea that the edge is the place to head for after you have gone through the hoop.

When passer and catcher work together it is easier to make a longer trip. Be sure to start the baby deep enough

and make the push strong enough to cover the whole distance. Bumping your head on a hoop doesn't hurt, but it

can be startling. To prevent such a contact, the catcher must be on hand to pull the swimmer through under the rim if he begins to surface too fast.

By this time the baby has had enough experience underwater to know what to do with his arms if he wants to remain stable. A child who has been through the hoop many times will start to use his hands to hurry him along. Once this happens, a second hoop should be placed about a foot ahead of the first. Success with two hoops lies in the

depth and force of the send-off as well as the baby's propulsion power. When he can get through two hoops easily, either add a third or place the second a little further away and a little nearer the surface. Eventually he will be able to get through several hoops placed at different angles and wend his way through a corridor of plastic rings. By that time he will have the chest and shoulders, lungs and heart, back and legs that an athlete would envy.

Make It Work

A poor teacher cannot turn out a good program in the best of situations. A good one can do a fine job in a made-over coal cellar. It isn't what you learned in school, it's what you are. The poor teacher goes by the book forever. The good teacher may get her first ideas from the book, but every idea gives her a new one of her own. The first balance beam was a fence, the trampoline a bed, the hockey rink a pond in the woods.

If something floats, any good teacher will throw it into the pool and see what the kids will do with it. If it sinks, the good teacher will throw it into the pool and see if the kids will dive for it. And if it is something that can hang half in and half out, like the plastic and metal bench pictured here, the good teacher will make an improvised

slide and watch the kids go for it. Every child in the place will love to zip down its slippery surface and be caught by a waiting mermaid.

Down with Water Wings

When I was little, children used water wings, which were totally unreliable. There was no way to tie them on and half the time they floated away when we weren't looking.

Since those days just about every kind of flotation device, from plastic tables with chair slings (might as well stay home in the high chair) to complete life jackets (which buckle four ways but aren't much good unless they bear the Coast Guard seal of approval), has been manufactured.

There are tires that go around middles, and a child can slip right down through the hole with never a sound. There are also inflatable armbands that always stay on top even when the baby has gone to the bottom. There are tin cans, plastic bottles, and rubber balls that can be tied onto little backs and look like a good base for a bustle. All of these gadgets help somebody, mostly the manufacturer. If anything can give a mother a false sense of security, it's a flotation device. A child learning to swim with such aids is in the same predicament as the child who has training wheels on his bike, he has to learn twice.

Sometimes a busy teacher working with older children who did not learn to swim as babies will tie flotation devices of one kind or another around the waists of several pupils while she gives her attention to one. These floats supposedly guarantee their safety, but nothing guarantees safety in the water short of knowing how to swim. It is far wiser to teach children without any such aids, keeping in mind at all times that they can't swim and that you are totally responsible for them until they can.

In the Harness

There is one flotation device, however, that can be recommended unreservedly. It comes with one perfectly reliable floater, the mother. In order to give the child the feeling of swimming freely with his head out of water

(he does fine face down), you can use a harness. Pin a small towel or a diaper around the child's chest. By hooking one hand into the towel at the child's back, you can give him just enough support so his back muscles will hold up his head. One hand is then free to help with arm and leg motion. Once he begins to dog paddle, a length of nylon cord can be slipped through the harness to give the swimmer even more freedom. Be sure that the assisting support is barely enough to meet the need and no more. It will be needed less and less until finally the need may be only psychological. At that time just wearing the harness seems to be enough. Don't argue. Tie it on and let him go. One day he'll simply forget it and be totally free.

The harness has another use. It is very effective when the family goes to the beach and the mother doesn't feel competent in water herself. Rather than make yourself (and the child) nervous with a constant stream of don'ts, harness him to thirty feet of light nylon line and let him go on in and find out what swimming at the beach is like. If danger threatens or it's time to go home, you can always reel him in. Such seagoing leashes also make it possible for small children to swim from boats when they are taken along on water outings.

One lesson which should be included in any course for children who live near the sea is how to use a life jacket properly. A teacher named Sally, who lives in Maine, where the water is not only very available but very cold, teaches even the smallest how to hold their heads up should they be washed overboard in a life jacket. One of her little swimmers proved the merit of her preventive measures. He was swept from the stern of his grandfather's fishing boat and it took ten minutes of maneuvering in a choppy sea before he could be picked up. His only comment was "I held my head up for Sally." Did you ever feel that you didn't have very much value to offer? Most people do at one time or another; Sally shouldn't.

22
THE HIGH DIVE

It is a long time since that first day when the baby was handed to his mother as she stood waist-deep in water. She can even go up and down the ladder with her baby under one arm. Now it's time to teach the *fall-in*, which will remove the last danger of surprise should the child fall into the water unaccompanied and unprotected.

The Fall-In

The baby sits on the edge of the pool and the "catcher" stands close by in the water. It would be well to keep ready hands near but not on the little body. There is no danger ahead in the water, but there is behind from a bump on the head if laughter should tip him over. The well-known phrase "Here we go, one, two, three, *down*" is spoken and gentle hands tip the little fellow into the water. Let him go down and try to control your impatience. When he has gone as far as his weight can take him, he will start up. If you are the anxious type, have someone sitting on the bottom wearing a mask. She will be able to

see what you cannot see, the baby's expression. If he is overlong in surfacing, give him a little help with a push, but don't hurry. He knows where up is and who's up there. And he knows how to get there.

I once watched the baby of friends fall into a hotel patio pool in Cuernavaca. As he disappeared his distraught father behaved just as I had when my daughter Petie went in so long ago. He raced across the lawn kicking off his shoes as he went. His wife, who had recently enrolled their son in a baby-swim program, was unperturbed. "Wait," she told him, "you have your watch on. He'll be right up . . . just wait." Sure enough, when the fall had run its course, up he came and when his head broke the surface his mother reached in and pulled him out. The baby was full of sorrow—his diapers were wet. As soon as he was stripped of their soggy weight and had calmed down his mother sat him on the edge and tipped him in again. This time there were no howls of dismay as he rose. He had that nice clean free feeling he had come to associate with being in water. Be sure when your baby cries that you know the *real* reason, not the one you think it is.

Unassisted Fall-In

After the baby has done the fall-in several times with your assistance, try for a little cooperation. Back off about four feet and repeat the "Here we go . . ." Do not count on immediate action. The baby may suffer from a certain amount of indecision. Have an assistant right there to help him over the first few trips he must take on his own. When he arrives, go down together a few times and be sure that love and laughter are the rewards.

If you have no handy assistants and are doing your baby coaching alone, you may have to pull the baby in with you the first few times. Make it exciting, because it *is*. Falling or jumping into water is quite a different sensation

from just being in water. Such an adventure may have lost the power to thrill you because you have done it so often. To understand the baby's feeling imagine yourself standing on a fifty foot diving tower. Your best friend, a

channel swimmer, takes your hand and you jump. You
know you are safe, but it's scary all the same. It's scary, it's
exciting, it's *wow!* One of the nicest things about being
around babies is that you are in on so many firsts. Do you
remember his face when you gave him his first taste of
orange juice?

When you have given each child a little personal help with their *fall-in*, line the class up for a group trip. Have the mothers set their children right on the edge, where it will be easier to tip over into the water. The child who is sitting way back is inclined to stay there even if the others take off without him.

Some little people go in yelling. Those are the same ones who later will yell all the way down the ski hill. If the mother adds to the excitement with a huge *wheeeeeeeeeee!* of her own, what might start out as protest can be turned into enthusiasm.

Siamese Jumping

There is often one little fellow who just can't bring himself to go along with the crowd. He will remain sitting while loudly lamenting the others' desertion of him. Next time the class goes in, sit beside him and go in with him. He may need a little reinforcing, which is quite different from forcing. As you surface, give him an extra ration of hugs and praise. Then when you hand him back to his mother, tell her how wonderful he was. She for her part does the same and the next few times she should go in with him. It's fun for everybody, and you can do *siamese jumping* from every part of the pool.

Setting Up Stations

If you are using a backyard pool, you may be able to use the pool steps for many adventures. If you start the older children jumping off from the top step, they will invariably use it as an intermediate step before they really let go and fall in. Don't let them get too used to this easier way. The emergency fall is rarely taken from a convenient step. Set up stations. The first jump-in can be off the steps, but the second is over where the drain "talks." The third is from the other side of the pool where the toy duck is sitting.

It even helps to have a different catcher for each station. The grandmother is next to the talking drain. The teacher will take the deep-water jump. Once jumping in becomes routine it will not be the jump that causes the newness and excitement, it will be the catcher that makes it different.

Off the Board

Once children (of any age) are used to going off the edge sitting, standing, alone, or in company, it's time to use the diving board. Children like to jump on beds, sofas, and trampolines. It's another sensation of freedom. Take your child out to the end of the diving board and do a few bounces. It will *feel* good. Then pause for a second, say the magic words "Here we go, one, two, three, *down*," and jump. Go down as far as you can with the child held close and then kick to the surface. When this stunt becomes familiar, release him underwater and let him kick himself back up. The teenage assistants at the YMCA in Leominster, Massachusetts, take the babies down to the bottom at the deep end and sit with them for a few seconds before surfacing. When the babies are old enough to grasp what they see, they will bring up poker chips which are tossed in just before the jump.

Out on His Own

Getting out of the pool is the last step in "waterproofing" a baby and depends on his age, the height of the deck, and the size of his tummy. Most babies have trouble getting their tummies over *anything*, so you can feel pretty proud of the baby and yourself if he can surface and propel himself to an edge and hold on. One young teenager, hired to waterproof a young baby in his own backyard pool, found the ladder just too much for his pupil. The baby's lessons had been started because a baby cousin had drowned in a wading pool and the mother was terrified for her own baby. The teenager reminded himself that he had been

asked to make the baby water-safe, and after a few weeks the baby could fall in, surface, and make it to the ladder. But there was no way in which he could climb that ladder. While he was clutching the step one day the boy was overlong in lifting him out. The frustrated baby set up such a howl that neighbors from two houses away came on the run to find out what was wrong. There hung the baby, red in the face and yelling for help. There sat the teenager, a smile of satisfaction on his face. He had done what he had set out to do. That baby wouldn't drown anywhere with his lung power and his ability to hang on.

Edging Up

As soon as the baby begins to make progress both underwater and on top and can propel himself even a few feet, edge him in the direction of the pool's side. As he paddles

on in the right direction, be ready to cushion his head when he touches base. You want to make the side a goal not a peril. As he reaches it, pull his hands forward to grab it. Once he has his hands on the lip he will pull himself up and test it for information with his mouth. A button nose showing above the side of the pool should be cause for much celebration, praise, and love.

As lesson follows lesson and the side is reached but the climb-out is still too difficult, use the baby's mother as bait. The ability to make the climb may still be far off, but the idea that it is the ultimate goal will be stored for future reference.

Up and Out

The time when he can get out on his own will depend, of course, on the baby's age and the height of the deck.

But one day with just a little help, say one foot in the drain and one little push, your baby will be a graduate. That's the day to have a party. It's always nice to have a reason to celebrate. It's always nice to be recognized, and it's especially nice to be the mother of a child who has accomplished something. The swimming baby is special and will probably give you that pleasure many times.

23
NATURE'S
POOLS

There it lies glittering in the sun. Breezes ruffle its surface and if you lean way out from the dock you can see minnows nibbling at the pilings. Sometimes there are pretty stones down there or a flower might float by just out of reach. It *looks* like water, it *smells* like water, and it *feels* like water. Why not go in and see if it *is* water? So he does. What can you do about it? You can teach him to swim in that water and to get out of that water.

Lake, bay, and river swimming present slightly different problems from those of man-made pools. There may not be a precipitous drop at the edge, but that doesn't mean there isn't one waiting ten feet further out. The pool is one big danger but you can see it all at a glance, both the surface and the bottom. Natural water holes may be shallow and safe in one spot but deep and dangerous a few feet away. You can't always see what's floating on the surface if the sun is in your eyes and you can hardly ever see what's on the bottom. So if you live near the water, visit friends near the water, or vacation near the water, waterproofing the baby is a must. There are a few things you should take into con-

siteration, however, before you begin to teach a baby to swim in a lake, bay, or river.

All in Good Time

Don't rush the season. Let the water warm up enough so that everyone can enjoy more than just a few shivery minutes without all concentration focusing on one sensation: *cold*. The shallows are warmer than the deeper spots, and if there is a spring feeding the lake, it will be colder near the spring. Little coves are warmer than open shores along bays or rivers.

At Bottom

Your little person has very communicative feet and they tell his brain all sorts of nice things. They have learned from the floor, the rug, the cement walk, the brick patio, and the lawn that there are different "feels" to things. Once in the mud of the lake or the sand of the bay, they send up a dozen messages at once. Mother's feet, which have lost contact with almost everything but shoe soles, may be very uncommunicative most of the time, but wait till they get in a river bottom! The mud that pleases the baby so much is full of terror for many mothers. It is full of wiggly things. They can't see them and they can't identify them. But they can certainly tell the world (and the baby) about them.

Babies are quite fearless when they are new. True, they don't want to be dropped, which means they have good sense. They don't like loud noises, which means they are sensitive. But until someone teaches them, they are not afraid of caterpillars, mice, fish, snakes, spiders, worms, or wiggly things in mud. Most of nature's creatures are not out to punish humans and will let alone what lets them alone. You can probably count on one hand the number of times you have been stung by a bee, but how many times have you seen someone get hysterical because a bee alighted on his picnic plate? We usually attract what we fear. The skier who is afraid of falling, falls. The child balancing on a fence who *knows* he can't make it to the end, doesn't make it. The person slashing wildly at a bee, gets stung. Someone had to teach that skier, that fence walker, that bee thrasher to tense with fear. The time such negative conditioning really takes is when a person is very young and does not yet have enough experience to make up his own mind.

So if you are afraid of wiggly things in the mud, make up your mind before you go into the lake with your baby that silence is golden and self-control is the key to your child's success. You will find after you have had some experience with squashing panic that there wasn't anything to be afraid of after all. And you may wonder, in passing, who scared *you*. If you are tenderfooted, wear a pair of old tennis shoes. But don't be afraid of the bottom.

An Ounce of Prevention

You will need to take certain precautions for sensitive skin. If you or the baby tend to attract insect life, use one of the many bug repellents for protection. The sun on water burns skin much faster than the same sun in your garden. And don't be deceived by half-cloudy days; you can get a burn then, too. Use some of the screening lotion that keeps out most of the ultraviolet rays but still permits a protecting tan to appear.

If you are taking the baby into a bay, keep in mind that the water will be salty. It won't bother the baby's eyes, but if he has a diaper rash it will bother his bottom very much when he first goes in. While it would probably be good for the rash, it will sting and his computer may store the message, *water—hurt*. So cover the rash with a good waterproof ointment before you go in.

Lesson Time

The lesson plan is the same as the one for the pool, with a few variations. When it is time to teach falling-in, you will need a low dock or a raft. A board held steady by two friends can approximate a pool edge if nothing more solid is available. And when it comes to getting out, it will be a cinch. There is no cumbersome pool lip to contend with. Once you have taught the baby to swim for shore, he can usually clamber up the gentle incline by himself.

Don't be afraid to take the baby swimming in the rain. You will find that the water is warmer than the air and the raindrops make interesting patterns. And don't be afraid of the dark. If the night is hot and you think a dip would make *you* feel better, take the baby along—and afterward hold him close to you in your blanket while you watch August stars fall. Night is full of magic, not bogey men, and the way to teach that is to go out in it, enjoy it, and fill your heart with it. Remember: what you feel, your baby feels. What feels nicer than a moonlit night?

The Picnic

Swimming makes people hungry, so take a lunch with you. If the baby is very little lunch may consist of breast milk or a bottle, but if he is beginning to eat what you eat, just what is that? Babies will eat what is given to them, and the tastes that are developed will stay with them forever. That's why Mexican kids like tacos, Eskimo kids like fish, Italian kids like pasta, German kids like sauerbraten—and American kids like hot dogs, hamburgers, potato chips, and soda pop. The tacos are made from flour that has not been robbed of its nutrients, the fish is loaded with vitamins and minerals, the pasta is also made from whole-grain flour, and the sauerbraten hasn't been injected and treated chemically. Hot dogs, on the other hand, can contain over thirty percent fat (not to mention the high cereal content), and the bun is as good as paper. Hamburgers are similarly high in fat, and chips can put three pounds on you in one evening, as their salt causes you to retain water. Soda pop and cola contain artificial flavoring, dyes, and often a good shot of caffein. Would you give a two-year-old a cup of coffee?

Your baby is new to this world. If you want the best of all possible houses for what's on the inside, take pains with his diet. Just as he must depend on you to teach him to save his life in water, he must depend on you to make that life worth living by giving him a strong, healthy, attractive body.

24
EVERYBODY SWIM

We have seen how swimming helps to build strong, healthy bodies, fosters self-confidence, and encourages the spirit of adventure. Swimming has other benefits as well. It is, for example, extremely therapeutic. Consider its effect on the handicapped.

What Is a Handicap?

Everybody is handicapped one way or another. We all have areas in which we are not as strong or secure as others. Some handicaps show and some do not.

There are people who are not as smart as others, but perhaps they make up for it by being able to enjoy every hour of every day. Some people are highly intelligent but have trouble getting along with other people. There are people who have marvelous figures but lack coordination, and others who are so fat they can scarcely get out of their chairs, yet once on their feet they are light and graceful.

A Common Ground

Little children have handicaps, too. There are some whose muscles don't obey them when they want to make a simple, coordinated movement, like putting one foot ahead of the other. There are some who can't hear well, some who don't see well, and others who don't talk or even think as well as other children. But they all have one thing in common with "normal" children—they can all *swim*.

Whether normal or handicapped, all children have a need to release tension through physical activity. It's hard to get enough physical outlets if you can't walk, hear, see, or think well, because you can't participate in most sports —you don't perform well. When you perform badly you begin to feel badly.

But anybody who does *something* well—like swimming —feels good about himself, even if it is only once a week. And anybody who feels good about himself once a week has a good chance of finding something else to like about himself. Regular encouragement builds dividends.

Teach Them to Swim

Anybody who can teach babies to swim can teach a handicapped child. It takes the same qualities. You have to be kind and patient and you need hands that talk. The best time to start teaching a handicapped child is in babyhood. When he's a baby he doesn't know he's handicapped, and he has not developed all kinds of wrong motions that have to be worked around and sometimes unlearned.

The baby who is blind doesn't need to see his mother in the water. He can feel her close, and her hands feel just as good to him as the hands of any mother on any baby. The deaf baby is no different than the baby who doesn't understand language yet. He gets his information non-verbally and is particularly good at it because that's all he has to rely on. He also appreciates the vibration of humming and singing. Water helps the baby who cannot control his muscles. When he's on dry land there is nothing to resist his erratic movement, but in the water there is something to push against.

If you can manage it, try to put handicapped babies in with nonhandicapped babies. All babies take on the color of the group, and the handicapped one will too. He will make much faster progress than if he had to wait until he was older and then was segregated. Nobody likes to be segregated. The other babies won't know if one of their number has a physical disadvantage.

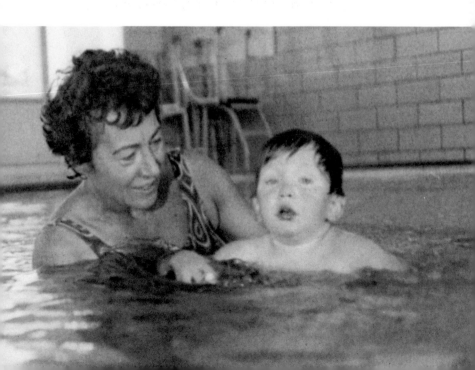

A Chance to Be Free

How wonderful it is for a handicapped baby to be free from the things that tie him in knots. Water may not make him the equal of every other baby, but it makes him much more equal than he would be anywhere else. And it is giving him a chance to improve and to become more like other children. It is also giving his mother a chance to see him happy and behaving more like other babies. It's giving her a chance to get out among other women, to talk, to share, to laugh a little. Mothers don't like to be segregated either.

Water and Relaxation

There is another therapeutic benefit to swimming—the simple joy of relaxation. Grown-ups often find it hard to relax. Subject to stress in its many forms, they start to

tighten certain muscle groups early in the morning with the breakfast rush or commuter traffic. By evening those muscles will be tight and often painful, causing backache, shoulder pain, stiff necks, and headaches. If stomach muscles are involved there may be cramping, at best a vague discomfort that may be mistaken for hunger.

The baby, too, suffers from stress, but his discomfort is more general than that of his parents. He becomes restless and cries. When he falls asleep he is fitful. He simply has not had enough *physical* outlet to offset the stresses under which he lives.

Relieving the Stress

The best way to offset tension is with physical activity. The baby can't run down to the Y for a game of handball or join a gym class. He can't even put on a record and gyrate to rock or take a walk around the block. He has to depend on his mother. If she reads a handbook on bringing up babies and stops with the directions for heating bottles, changing diapers, and taking a temperature, the baby will be the loser. But if she is up on the latest word on babies, she will say to herself, "My baby, like every other living creature, needs to move. How can I arrange for him to get what he needs *besides* his meals, lodging, clothing, and me?" If she does arrange for his other needs, the baby and the family will have a better life.

Back to the Water

The surest and best way to exercise a baby is in the water, because there he is already an adept. He had to start on the day he was born to adapt to the world of air and sun-light. But water, that's different. One-third of the most important months of his entire life were spent in it, and he knows how to use it. Water will take all the energy he has to give, just as a game in the Orange Bowl will take all each contestant has to give. The best and most complete relaxation comes after you have given *physically* all there is to give.

So teach your baby to swim. Not only will he be strong, healthy, and self-assured, he will be relaxed and happy. What greater gifts can you give?

APPENDIX

Are baby-swim classes a passing fad? No they are not. What has been done by swimming parents for their own children and by swimming teachers for many children can now be done by any mother who will take the time. Both that mother and the teacher who takes on classes at the Y, club, school, motel, or summer colony on the lake, bay, or river will run into questions. They will be the same questions we at the Institute for Physical Fitness have run into for fifteen years. To supply answers other than our own, we sent out hundreds of questionnaires to other baby-swim programs. The replies have been very helpful in putting together this book, and we pass them on to you in the hope that they will make your way a little easier.

Fifty percent of the replies came from YMCAs, thirty-eight percent from YWCAs, six percent from YMCA-YWCAs, and six percent from park and recreation and private programs. Forty-seven percent of the questionnaires were returned from eastern states, forty-one percent from the Midwest, and six percent each from the Far West and Canada. The greatest concentration was in Indiana and Illinois, followed by Connecticut, Massachusetts, and Pennsylvania. Here are the results:

What Did Your Organization Think of This Idea in the Beginning?

Fifty-two percent of the organizations were negative. Forty-eight percent were positive. Some of the responses were as follows:

Positive (32%): "Wonderful," "Enthusiastic," "Interested," "Great."

Mildly Positive (16%): "We'll try," "Receptive," "Interested," "Good," "O.K.," "It may be good public relations," "Willing."

Mildly Negative (29%): "Scared," "Doubted it would work," "No interest," "Reluctant," "Wary," "Skeptical," "Don't like it," "Hesitant," "Not much."

Very Negative (23%): "Very negative," "Feared pollution," "Dangerous."

It would seem that when the organizations liked the idea they liked it very much. Those who were negative were equally vociferous. The teachers who instituted these programs in the face of such objections have been both courageous and persuasive.

What Does Your Organization Think Now?

Ninety percent positive and ten percent mildly positive. No organization remained negative. Tests taken before and after the baby-swim program proved that there was no sign of pollution and that objection was withdrawn. One very negative organization that is now in the mildly positive group approved because they needed the revenue. Every organization has increased the number of classes it serves and most have long waiting lists.

All groups report serving hundreds of children each year and some, many thousands. The Boston YWCA has a record of 6,787 in the last few years. The Harvey YMCA in Chicago has taught an average of 1,600 children a year for the past six years.

What Is the Most Popular Starting Age?
Six months with three months not far behind.

Do You Incorporate Gym Classes with the Swim Classes?
Sixty-six percent do hold gym classes prior to the swim either in a separate area or on the deck. They feel it adds considerably to the program. Gym usually lasts from twenty minutes to half an hour and the swim program a half-hour.

How Long Do You Keep Your Babies?
Most children stay with the swim classes for at least two or three complete sessions, some continue until they are old enough to go into classes for older children. If they last past the first two classes, they usually stay.

Number of Weeks per Session?
Most sessions run for ten weeks, some for six and eight weeks, a very few for five (not too much can be achieved in this short time), and a few for over fourteen. It is my thought that longer sessions should be held in winter since absences are higher during that season.

Those attending classes once a week took an average of ten lessons. Those attending twice a week took an average of sixteen lessons. Many also attended family-night swims and special weekend swims, especially those who had more than one child in the family.

*Do the Mothers Come to Your Organization the First
Time for Themselves or for Their Babies?*

Most come at first to get their babies into swim classes.
Many join women's classes later.

Has the Baby Program Been a Financial Success?

Only two replies were negative. One of those replies was
from Canada where the charge is ten cents per class with
the government making up the deficit, the other from a
Y charging fifty-five cents per class. Most public organizations charge between one and two dollars per class, one
went as high as three-fifty and has a long waiting list.
Private organizations go as high as five dollars a class
payable in advance for sixteen lessons, and also have long
waiting lists. It is a mistake to undercharge the mother
and a mistake to underpay the baby-swim instructor.
Those who are both successful and underpaid have found
they can start their own classes elsewhere so long as they
have passed the Red Cross Water Safety Instructor test.

Clothing?

Most organizations recommend that babies wear little
swim suits or training pants. Eleven percent permit only
diapers and rubber pants. Many teaching in their own
pools and out-of-doors encourage complete nudity.

Screamers?

An average of twenty-eight percent of the babies are
screamers during the first three weeks; then there is com-
parative quiet. The loudest age is two and the louder sex,
boys.

How Was Your Program Publicized?

Newspapers   90%
Radio spots   41%

Word of mouth   34%
Brochures   31%
TV spots   24%
Flyers   24%
Letters to members   10%
Letters to clubs   10%
Flyers to hospitals   7%
Brochures to La Leche League   3%
Distribution via diaper services   3%

Massachusetts seems to have the departments of obstetrics on her side in many hospitals. The teacher of prenatal exercises in one such department signs the babies up before they arrive, and another hospital cooperates with a baby-swim group that sends membership cards to all new arrivals.

At the YMCA in Leominster, Massachusetts, the Lions Club, which comes to observe, has become a highly efficient publicity agent. If there is one thing men understand it is sports, and once they have seen the baby swimmers in action, they are sold.

Attitude toward Observers?

Most classes allow observers, but seventeen percent do not, because they feel it distracts. My experience is that nothing really distracts a swimming baby. Some prefer to limit the spectators but all open their doors to swimming instructors. Sixty percent report that their programs have been copied by other organizations, and many are besieged by college students doing papers.

Employment of Teenagers?

Most groups use teenage help when it is available, usually during the summer months. One organization provides an opportunity for college students to get credit in psychology courses by assisting with the babies. Only one organization reported them to be unreliable and immature. All other reports were positive.

Enrollment of Handicapped Children?

Fifty percent have handicapped children in the program and all report that they have been successful.

Attitude of the Medical Profession?

Seventy percent of the doctors questioned in each area were in favor of the program. Young doctors were particularly enthusiastic. Most pediatricians heartily approved. Doctors who themselves exercise seem to be the best backers. Several have sent in letters of approval with permission to publish. Fourteen percent disapprove, especially during virus season.

Has It Been Worth It?

All organizations reported that it was. The children grow in strength and flexibility and seem to be superior to other children when they advance to toddler and tiny tot classes. They have more self-confidence and self-control and they are all water-wise as well. Their posture is well above average and most go on with their swim programs and work their way onto teams. Many of these children exhibit leadership qualities and are very dependable. One teacher says, "Every morning of the week our pool is filled with happy moms and adorable babies . . . what better way to start a teaching day?"

INDEX

ABOUT
THE AUTHOR

Bonnie Prudden, well-known lecturer, author, and TV personality, is an authority in the field of physical fitness and has helped to make thousands of babies water-safe with her baby-swim programs in YMCAs and YWCAs across the country. A young and vigorous grandmother of sixty, the author lives and works in Stockbridge, Massachusetts, where she is director of The Bonnie Prudden Institute of Physical Fitness.